Geometry

Practice
Workbook

Houghton Mifflin Harcourt

Printed in the U.S.A.

ISBN   978-0-544-71633-9
1 2 3 4 5 6 7 8 9 10   0928   24 23 22 21 20 19 18 17 16 15
4500541263   A B C D E F G

Contents

Student Worksheets

LESSON 1-1

Segment Length and Midpoints

Practice and Problem Solving: A/B

Use a straightedge and a compass to construct a segment of length $AB + CD$.

1.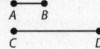

2.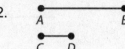

Use the distance formula to determine whether each pair of segments have the same length.

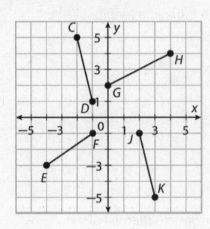

3. $\overline{CD}$ and $\overline{EF}$

4. $\overline{GH}$ and $\overline{JK}$

Determine the coordinates of the midpoint for each segment. Identify the quadrant that each midpoint lies in.

5. $\overline{PQ}$ has endpoints $P(5, -3)$ and $Q(2, 4)$.

6. $\overline{RS}$ has endpoints $R(-2, 3)$ and $S(-8, -2)$.

Midpoint: _____

Midpoint: _____

Quadrant: _____

Quadrant: _____

LESSON
1-1

Segment Length and Midpoints

Practice and Problem Solving: C

Use a straightedge and a compass to construct a segment that has the given length.

A   B   C   D

1. $AB + 2(CD)$

2. $2(AB) - CD$

Answer the following questions about the lengths of the segments on the grid. Use the distance formula to justify each answer.

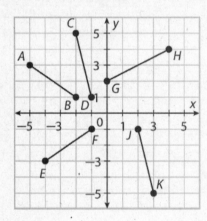

3. $\overline{CD}$ and _____ have the same length.

4. $\overline{EF}$ and _____ have the same length.

5. _____ has a different length than all of the other segments on the grid.

Given triangle *ABC*, determine the coordinates of the vertices of a new triangle formed by the midpoints of each side of triangle *ABC*.

6. $A(-1, -3)$, $B(4, -1)$, $C(3, 4)$

$M_{\overline{AB}}$ (_____, _____)

$M_{\overline{BC}}$ (_____, _____)

$M_{\overline{CA}}$ (_____, _____)

7. $A(4, -4)$, $B(0, 4)$, $C(-3, -1)$

$M_{\overline{AB}}$ (_____, _____)

$M_{\overline{BC}}$ (_____, _____)

$M_{\overline{CA}}$ (_____, _____)

LESSON
1-2

Angle Measures and Angle Bisectors

Practice and Problem Solving: A/B

Construct a copy of each angle.

1.

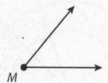

2.

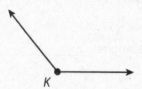

Use a compass and a straightedge to construct the bisector of each angle.

3.

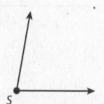

4.

5.

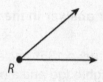

6. Explain how you can use a straightedge and a protractor to show that each angle you formed by a bisector is one-half the original angle.

_____

_____

Determine the measure of each angle. Then describe each angle as acute, right, obtuse, or straight.

7.

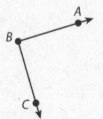

8.

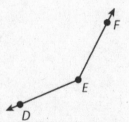

9.

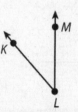

m∠ABC = _____

m∠DEF = _____

m∠KLM = _____

_____

_____

_____

LESSON 1-2

Angle Measures and Angle Bisectors

Practice and Problem Solving: C

Use the figure for Problems 1–3.

1. Name the obtuse angle. _____

2. Name two acute angles. _____

3. Name two right angles. _____

4. Keisha has a straightedge and a compass, but no protractor. What kind of angle can Keisha draw exactly with only these tools?

_____

Draw your answer in the space provided.

5. Construct a 135° angle using only a straightedge and a compass.

6. An acute angle measures $(6x - 45)°$. Write an inequality to describe the range of all possible values of x. _____

Use only a compass, a straightedge, and the angle shown to construct an angle with the new measure that is given.

7. 21°

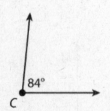

8. 32°

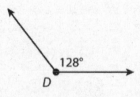

9. $\overrightarrow{DF}$ bisects $\angle CDE$, $\overrightarrow{DG}$ bisects $\angle FDE$, and $\angle CDG = 51°$. Find

m$\angle CDE$. _____

10. m$\angle XWY$ is twice $\angle XWZ$. Explain whether $\overrightarrow{WZ}$ must be the angle bisector of $\angle XWZ$.

LESSON 1-3

Representing and Describing Transformations

Practice and Problem Solving: A/B

1. Use coordinate notation to describe the transformation of $\triangle PQR$.

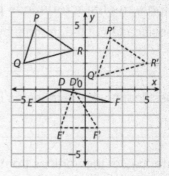

$P(-4, 5)$ → $P'($ _____ , _____ $)$

$Q(-5, 2)$ → $Q'($ _____ , _____ $)$

$R(-1, 3)$ → $R'($ _____ , _____ $)$

2. Describe the algebraic rule for $\triangle DEF$.

$(x, y) \rightarrow$ $($ _____ , _____ $)$

Name the transformation described by the given rule.

3. $(x, y) \rightarrow (-x, y)$

_____

4. $(6, 2) \rightarrow (-6, -2)$

_____

5. $(5, 8) \rightarrow (8, -5)$

_____

6. $(x, y) \rightarrow (x + 9, y + 2)$

_____

Draw the image of each figure under the given transformation.

7. $(x, y) \rightarrow (x + 4, y - 5)$

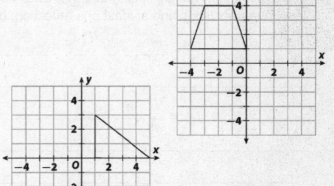

8. A 180° rotation around the origin

9. A reflection across the *y*-axis

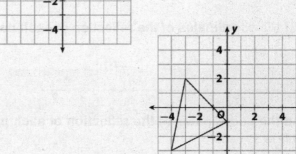

LESSON
1-3

Representing and Describing Transformations
Practice and Problem Solving: C

**A triangle undergoes a rigid motion on a coordinate plane. Tell
whether the given characteristic is preserved. Write Yes or No.**

1. The classification of the triangle by angles (obtuse, etc.)

   _____

2. The classification of the triangles by sides (scalene, etc.)

   _____

3. The distances of the vertices from the origin.

   _____

4. The orientation of the triangle with respect to the coordinate axes.

   _____

5. The area of the triangle

   _____

6. Triangle *A* has been mapped to Triangle *B* through a 180° rotation
   around the origin. Identify two other series of transformations that
   could also map Triangle *A* to Triangle *B*. Each series must include at
   least one translation and at least one reflection, but no rotations.

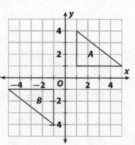

Find the coordinates of the reflection of each point across the line $x = 2$.

7. (5, 3)   8. (x, y)

   _____   _____

**Find the coordinates of the reflection of each point across
the line $y = -5$.**

9. (3, 4)   10. (x, y)

   _____   _____

LESSON 1-4

Reasoning and Proof

Practice and Problem Solving: A/B

Write a justification for each step. Choose from the following reasons.

Addition Property of Equality   Division Property of Equality

Segment Addition Postulate   Simplify

Substitution Property of Equality   Subtraction Property of Equality

1.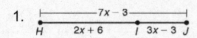

$HJ = HI + IJ$ _____

$7x - 3 = (2x + 6) + (3x - 3)$ _____

$7x - 3 = 5x + 3$ _____

$7x = 5x + 6$ _____

$2x = 6$ _____

$x = 3$ _____

Show that each conjecture is false by finding a counterexample.

2. For any integer n, $n^3 > 0$. _____

3. Each angle in a right triangle has a different measure.

   _____

Make a conjecture about each pattern. Then write the next two items.

4. 1, 2, 2, 4, 8, 32, . . .

   _____

   _____

5.

   _____

   _____

Name _____ Date _____ Class_____

Reasoning and Proof

Practice and Problem Solving: C

Solve. Write justifications for each step in your solution.

1. Solve for m∠3 in terms of m∠1. Write justifications for each step in your solution.

   Given: ∠1 and ∠2 are complementary.
             ∠2 and ∠3 are supplementary.

   _____ | _____
   _____ | _____
   _____ | _____
   _____ | _____

2. Explain logically how the Transitive Property of Equality can be derived from the Substitution Property of Equality and the Symmetric Property of Equality.

   _____

   _____

   _____

   _____

Make a conjecture about each pattern. Write the next two items.

3. −1, −8, −27, −64, . . .

   _____

4. 1, 11, 21, 1211, 111221, . . . (*Hint:* Try reading the numbers aloud in different ways.)

   _____

Determine if each conjecture is true. If not, write a counterexample.

5. If $a > b$ and $b > c$, then $a - b < a - c$.   _____

6. If n is an integer ($n \neq 0$), then $\frac{1}{n} > \left(\frac{1}{n}\right)^3$.   _____

Name _____ Date _____ Class_____

Translations
Practice and Problem Solving: A/B

Use the figure below to answer Problems 1–5.

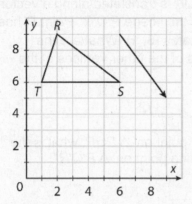

1. Triangle *RST* is translated along vector $\vec{v}$ to create the image *R'S'T'*. What are the coordinates of the vertices of the image?

   R' _____

   S' _____

   T' _____

2. What is the length of vector $\vec{v}$? What is the length of $\overline{RR'}$?

   _____ units   _____ units

3. If (*x*, *y*) is a point on △*RST*, what is the corresponding point on

   △*R'S'T'*? _____

4. Name vector $\vec{v}$ using component form. $\langle$ ___, ___ $\rangle$

5. Name a pair of parallel segments formed by vertices of the preimage

   and the image. _____ and _____

Use the figure below to answer Problems 6–8.

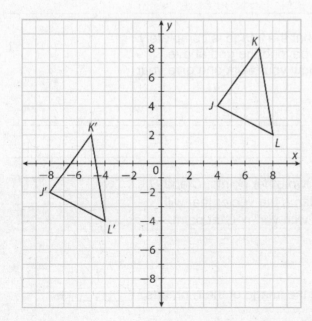

6. Triangle *J'K'L'* is the image of △*JKL* under a translation. Draw the translation vector $\vec{v}$ from *J* to its image in △*J'K'L'*. Write the vector in component form. $\langle$ ___, ___ $\rangle$

7. What is the slope of $\vec{v}$? _____

8. Triangle *J'K'L'* is also the image of △*DEF* under a translation along a vector $\langle -6,\ 4 \rangle$. Find the coordinates of points *D*, *E*, and *F*, and draw △*DEF*.

   D _____

   E _____

   F _____

Name _____ Date _____ Class_____

Translations
Practice and Problem Solving: C

Use the figure below to answer Problems 1–9.

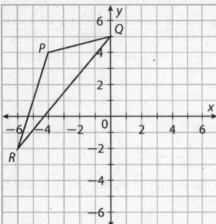

1. Triangle *PQR* is translated along a vector *v̄* to create the image *P'Q'R'*. Point *P'* has the coordinates (3, 1). What are the coordinates of the other vertices of the image?

   Q' _____ *R'* _____

2. If (*x*, *y*) is a point on △*PQR*, what is the corresponding point on △*P'Q'R'*?

   _____

3. Name vector *v̄* using component form.

   ⟨___ , ___⟩

4. Using the coordinates of the endpoints, find the slope of *PP'* and of *QQ'*.

   Slope of *PP'* ____ Slope of *QQ'* ____

5. What do the slopes of *PP'* and *QQ'* tell you about the lines?

   _____

6. What is the length of vector *v̄* (in radical form)? Explain your answer and show your work.

   _____

7. Suppose you want to translate △*PQR* so that the image is completely inside the fourth quadrant and does not go beyond the grid above. How long can the translation vector be? Show your work and give your answer as an inequality in radical form.

   _____

   _____

8. Plot points *A*(−10, −7) and *B*(−6, −4). Mark two other points, *C* and *D*, to make a rhombus in the third quadrant. Name the vector that will translate the rhombus to the first quadrant, with vertex *C'* at point

   (10, 9). ⟨___ , ___⟩

9. What will be the coordinates of vertex *D'* of the image of the rhombus? (___ , ___)

Name _____ Date _____ Class_____

Reflections

Practice and Problem Solving: A/B

Study the figures on the grid and answer the questions.

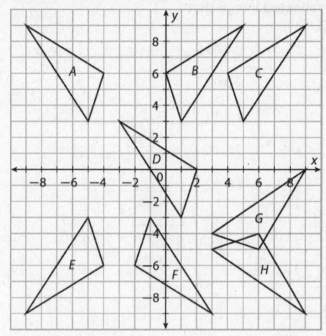

1. Which figure is the reflection of figure *A* over the *y*-axis? _____

2. Which two figures have *x* = −3 as their line of reflection? _____ and _____

3. Which figure is the reflection of figure *A* over the line *y* = *x*? _____

4. What is the equation of the line of reflection for figures *G* and *H*?

   _____

5. Which figures are **not** reflections of figure *A*? Name all. _____

Use principles of reflections to determine where to place the puck.

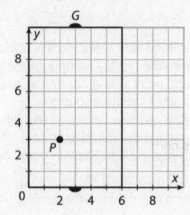

Mike is playing air hockey and wants to bounce the puck off the wall and into the goal at *G*(3, 10).

6. If the puck is at *P* (2, 3), what point on the right wall (*x* = 6) should he aim for? Sketch and label a figure on the grid. Explain your answer.

   _____

   _____

   _____

7. If the puck is at (0, 4), what point on the wall should he aim for?

   (_____ , _____)

8. If the puck is at (3, 2), what point on the wall should he aim for?

   (_____ , _____)

9. If the puck is at (3, 6), what point on the wall should he aim for?

   (_____ , _____)

LESSON
2-2

Reflections

Practice and Problem Solving: C

For each line of symmetry given, make constructions and/or do calculations to find the coordinates in the reflected image that correspond to (x, y) in the preimage, $\triangle ABC$.

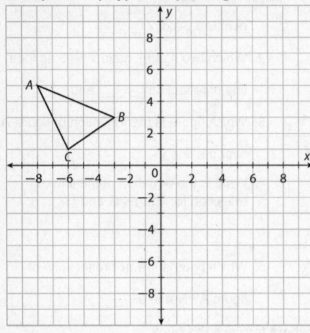

1. y-axis (_____ , _____)

2. x-axis (_____ , _____)

3. $x = 1$ (_____ , _____)

4. $y = -2$ (_____ , _____)

5. $y = x$ (_____ , _____)

6. $y = x - 2$ (_____ , _____)

Use principles of reflections to solve the problems.

7. The Beckwiths' driveway is lined with trees, so it is difficult to see cars approaching from the right. The dark black line represents the driveway, and point C is a car on the road. A mirror will be placed at point M at the end of the driveway, across the street. Draw and label a sketch to show the angle at which to place the mirror so that a person in the driveway can see the car. Explain your steps.

_____

_____

_____

8. Point $P(-2, -3)$ is reflected across line ℓ. Its image is point $Q(8, 12)$. Find the equation of line ℓ. Describe the steps you took.

$y = $ _____

_____

_____

LESSON 2-3 Rotations

Practice and Problem Solving: A/B

Follow the directions for Problems 1–5 to analyze rotations.

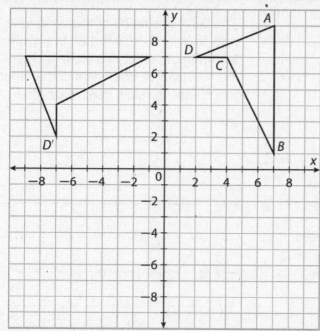

1. Draw a line from the origin, *O*, to point *D* and from *O* to *D'*. Measure the angle formed by $\overline{OD}$ and $\overline{OD}'$. How many degrees was figure

   ABCD rotated? ____ degrees

2. Find the coordinates of points on *ABCD* and corresponding points on its image. Label *A'*, *B'*, and *C'*.

   A(___, ___) *A'*(___, ___)

   B(___, ___) *B'*(___, ___)

   C(___, ___) *C'*(___, ___)

   D(___, ___) *D'*(___, ___)

   P(*x, y*) *P'*(_____ , _____)

3. If you rotate *A'B'C'D'* counterclockwise 90°, what is the sign of the

   x-coordinates of the new image? ____ Of the *y*-coordinates? ____

   In what quadrant is the new image? _____

4. Draw and label *A"B"C"D"*, the image of *A'B'C'D'* after being rotated 90° counterclockwise.

5. If (*x, y*) is a point on *ABCD,* what is its image on *A"B"C"D"*?

   (_____, _____)

Use principles of rotations to answer Problems 6–8.

6. What clockwise rotation produces the same image as a counterclockwise rotation of 220°? _____° clockwise

7. Tony Hawk was the first skateboarder to do a "900," a rotation of 900°. How many times did he rotate on the skateboard? _____ times

8. Each arm of this pinwheel is the image of another arm rotated around the center. What is the angle of rotation between one arm and the next? _____°

LESSON 2-3

Rotations

Practice and Problem Solving: C

Draw the rotations described in Problems 1–2.

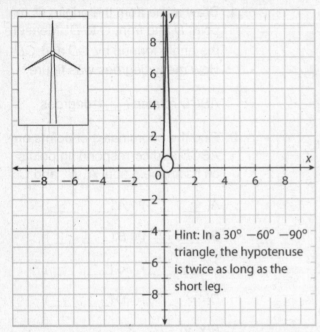

Hint: In a 30° −60° −90° triangle, the hypotenuse is twice as long as the short leg.

1. The tip of one blade of this wind turbine is at (0, 10). Rotate the blade to create the other two blades. Give the coordinates of the tips of the other two blades. Explain your reasoning.

   (___, ___) (___, ___)

   _____

   _____

   _____

   _____

   _____

2. Explain how to draw a rotation of △ABC 45° counterclockwise about point P without using a protractor to measure the angle. Mark the figure to show how to find one point of the image.

   _____

   _____

   _____

Use principles of rotations to answer Problems 3 and 4.

3. A figure in the first quadrant is rotated 180° about the origin. The same figure is reflected over the line y = −x. Both transformations produce images in the third quadrant. Under what conditions will the two transformations produce the same image? Explain your answer.

   _____

   _____

   _____

4. The hour hand and minute hand of a clock rotate around the center to show the time. At 12:00 the angle between the hands is 0°. Think about the angles of rotation for each hand during a given time period.

   Find the angle between the hands at 3:40. _____°

LESSON 2-4

Investigating Symmetry
Practice and Problem Solving: A/B

Use the figures on the grid to answer Problems 1–3.

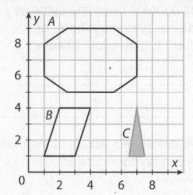

1. What are the equations of the lines of symmetry for figure *A*?

   _____

   _____

2. Does figure *B* have line symmetry, rotational symmetry, or both?

   _____

3. If you rotate figure *C* all the way around point (7, 4), 50° at a time, will you create a figure with rotational symmetry? Explain your answer.

   _____

Tell whether each figure appears to have line symmetry, rotational symmetry, both, or neither. If line symmetry, tell how many lines of symmetry. If rotational symmetry, give the angle of rotational symmetry.

4.   _____

   _____

5.   _____

   _____

6.   _____

   _____

7.   _____

   _____

Use principles of symmetry to answer Problems 8–9.

8. How many lines of symmetry does each quadrilateral have?

   isosceles trapezoid _____ rectangle with sides 2-4-2-4 _____

   square _____ rhombus _____

   parallelogram with sides 2-4-2-4 and angles ≠ 90° _____

9. How many lines of symmetry does a regular pentagon have? _____

   How many lines of symmetry does a regular hexagon have?_____

LESSON 2-4 Investigating Symmetry

Practice and Problem Solving: C

Use the figures on the grid to answer the questions about symmetry.

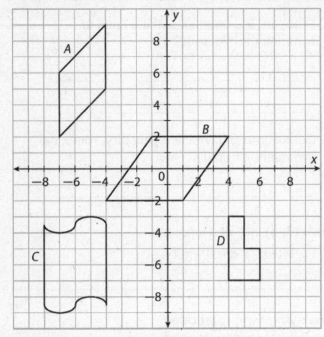

1. Does figure *A* have line symmetry, rotational symmetry, both, or neither? Explain your answer.

   _____

   _____

2. What are the equations of the lines of symmetry for figure *B*?

   $y =$ _____ $y =$ _____

3. What do the slopes of the lines tell you?

   _____

   _____

4. Describe the symmetry of figure *C*. _____

5. Describe a series of transformations that you could perform on figure *D* so that the figure and its image form a figure with rotational symmetry.

   _____

Use principles of symmetry to answer Problems 6–8.

6. How do you know that all regular polygons have both line symmetry and rotational symmetry?

   _____

7. If a rotation of 40° will map a symmetrical figure to itself, what other rotations will map the figure to itself? Name all up to 360°.

   _____

8. Name eight angle measures that can be angles of rotational symmetry.

   _____°, _____°, _____°, _____°, _____°, _____°, _____°, _____°.

   What characteristic do all angles of rotational symmetry have in common? Be specific.

   _____

LESSON 3-1

Sequences of Transformations

Practice and Problem Solving: A/B

Draw the image of △*ABC* after the given combination of transformations.

1. Translation along $\vec{V}$, then reflection across line ℓ

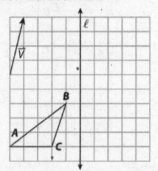

2. 180° rotation around point *P*, then translation along *W*

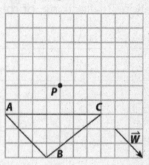

Rectangle *ABCD* is reflected across the *y*-axis, rotated 90° clockwise, and translated along the vector ⟨–6, 2⟩. Describe the effect on the figure.

3. Predict the effect of the first transformation.

_____

_____

_____

_____

4. Predict the effect of the second transformation.

_____

_____

_____

_____

5. Predict the effect of the third transformation.

_____

_____

_____

LESSON 3-1

Sequences of Transformations

Practice and Problem Solving: C

Solve.

1. Describe a sequence of three transformations that will result in a mapping of △ABC onto itself. Your sequence must include at least two different types of transformations (translations, reflections, or rotations).

   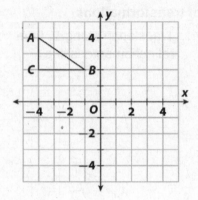

   _____

   _____

   _____

   _____

2. △EFG has vertices E(1, 5), F(0, –3), and G(–1, 2). △EFG is translated along the vector ⟨7,1⟩, and the image is reflected across the x-axis. What are the coordinates of the final image of G?

   _____

3. △KLM with vertices K(8, –1), L(–1, –4), and M(2, 3) is rotated 180° around the origin. The image is then translated. The final image of K has coordinates (–2, –3). What is the translation vector?

   _____

4. Point P has coordinates (a, b). Find the coordinates of P′, the image of P after a counterclockwise rotation of 90° around the origin, followed by reflection across the x-axis.

   _____

5. Point Q has coordinates (m, n). Find the coordinates of Q′, the image of Q after a rotation of 180° around the origin, followed by translation along the vector ⟨g, h⟩.

   _____

6. Describe a sequence of three transformations that will result in a mapping of rhombus ABCD onto rhombus A′B′C′D′. Your sequence must include one translation, one reflection, and one rotation.

   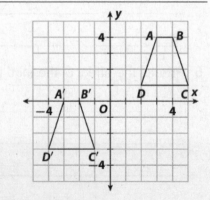

   _____

   _____

   _____

LESSON 3-2

Proving Figures are Congruent Using Rigid Motions

Practice and Problem Solving: A/B

Determine whether △ABC and △MNP are congruent. Explain your answer.

1.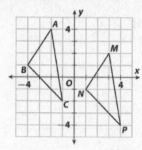

_____

_____

_____

2.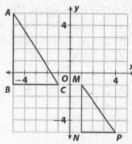

_____

_____

_____

_____

For each pair of congruent figures, specify a sequence of rigid motions that maps one figure onto the other.

3.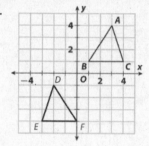

_____

_____

4.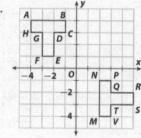

_____

_____

Decide if the angles or the segments in each pair are congruent. Write Yes or No.

5. ∠Q and ∠R

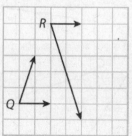

_____

6. $\overline{AB}$ and $\overline{CD}$

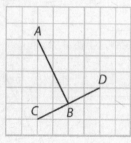

_____

7. $\overline{EF}$ and $\overline{GH}$

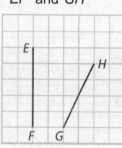

_____

8. ∠S and ∠T

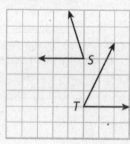

_____

LESSON 3-2

Proving Figures are Congruent Using Rigid Motions

Practice and Problem Solving: C

△ABC, with vertices A(1, 5), B(1, 2), and C(6, 1), is transformed in three steps. Describe each step as a translation, reflection, or rotation. If it is a translation, give the translation vector. If it is a reflection, give the line of reflection. If it is a rotation, give the angle of rotation. For each step, tell whether the transformed figure is congruent to △ABC.

1. **Step 1:** A'(1, –5), B'(1, –2), C'(6, –1)

   _____

2. **Step 2:** A"(–1, 5), B"(–1, 2), C"(–6, 1)

   _____

3. **Step 3:** A'"(2, –1), B'"(2, –4), C'"(–3, –5)

   _____

Describe the transformation or transformations of the top figure that will produce the image below it.

4.
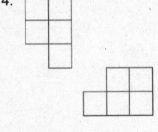

5.
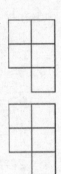

6.

_____   _____   _____

Identify the congruent pairs on the grid. Describe a series of transformations to prove each answer.

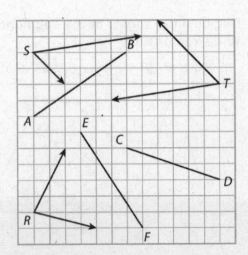

7. Congruent angles: _____

   _____

8. Congruent segments: _____

   _____

LESSON 3-3

Corresponding Parts of Congruent Figures are Congruent

Practice and Problem Solving: A/B

List all of the pairs of congruent angles and sides of the figures.

1. $\triangle KLM \cong \triangle GHI$

_____ $\cong$ _____   _____ $\cong$ _____

_____ $\cong$ _____   _____ $\cong$ _____

_____ $\cong$ _____   _____ $\cong$ _____

2. Rhombus $WXYZ \cong$ rhombus $DEFG$

_____ $\cong$ _____   _____ $\cong$ _____

_____ $\cong$ _____   _____ $\cong$ _____

_____ $\cong$ _____   _____ $\cong$ _____

_____ $\cong$ _____   _____ $\cong$ _____

Quadrilateral $ABCD \cong$ quadrilateral $EFGH$. In quadrilateral $ABCD$, $AB = 16$, $BC = 5w + 7$, $m\angle C = (2z - 1)°$, and $m\angle D = 50°$. In quadrilateral $EFGH$, $EF = 3y + 1$, $FG = 8$, $m\angle G = 80°$, and $m\angle H = (2x)°$. Find the value of the indicated variable.

3. Find the value of w.

_____

4. Find the value of x.

_____

5. Find the value of y.

_____

6. Find the value of z.

_____

Write the proof.

7. Given: Quadrilateral $MNPQ \cong$ quadrilateral $RSTU$; $\overline{MN} \cong \overline{PQ}$

   Prove: $\overline{MN} \cong \overline{TU}$

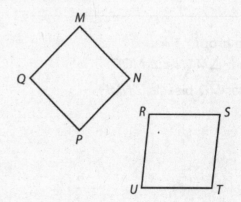

LESSON 3-3

Corresponding Parts of Congruent Figures are Congruent

Practice and Problem Solving: C

1. In rectangle *RSTU*, opposite sides have the same length, and *V* is the midpoint of $\overline{RT}$ and $\overline{SU}$. Find three different pairs of congruent triangles. Write a congruence statement for each pair.

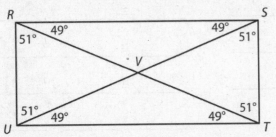

$\triangle ABC \cong \triangle EFG.$ **Write True or False for each statement. If the statement is false, explain why.**

2. The measure of $\angle A$ is 45°.

_____

3. The perimeter of $\triangle EFG$ is 32.

_____

4. $\triangle ABC$ is isosceles.

_____

5. The longest side of $\triangle EFG$ is $\overline{FE}$.

_____

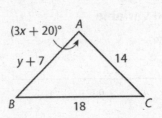

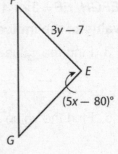

Write the proof.

6. Given: $\triangle MQN \cong \triangle MQP$

   Prove: $\overline{MQ}$ bisects $\angle NMP$

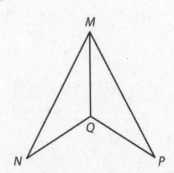

LESSON
4-1

Angles Formed by Intersecting Lines
Practice and Problem Solving: A/B

1. ∠PQR and ∠SQR form a linear pair. Find the sum of their measures. _____

2. Name the ray that ∠PQR and ∠SQR share. _____

Use the figures for Problems 3–8.

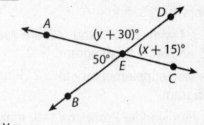

3. supplement of ∠AEB

4. complement of ∠AEB

5. $x =$ _____

6. $y =$ _____

7. m∠DEC = _____

8. m∠AED = _____

9. ∠DEF and ∠FEG are complementary. m∠DEF = $(3x - 4)°$, and
m∠FEG = $(5x + 6)°$.

Find the measures of both angles. _____

10. ∠DEF and ∠FEG are supplementary. m∠DEF = $(9x + 1)°$, and
m∠FEG = $(8x + 9)°$.

Find the measures of both angles. _____

Use the figure for Problems 11 and 12.

In 2004, several nickels were minted to commemorate the Louisiana
Purchase and Lewis and Clark's expedition into the American West. One
nickel shows a pipe and a hatchet crossed to symbolize peace between
the American government and Native American tribes.

11. Name a pair of vertical angles.

_____

_____

12. Name a linear pair of angles.

_____

13. ∠ABC and ∠CBD form a linear pair and have equal measures. Tell if

∠ABC is acute, right, or obtuse. _____

14. ∠KLM and ∠MLN are complementary. $\overline{LM}$ bisects ∠KLN. Find the

measures of ∠KLM and ∠MLN. _____

Angles Formed by Intersecting Lines

Practice and Problem Solving: C

Draw your answers in the space provided.

1. Draw two intersecting lines and label the resulting angles with the numbers 1, 2, 3, and 4.

2. Label $\angle 1$ with $x°$. $\angle 1$ and $\angle 2$ are supplementary. Find the measure of $\angle 2$ and label the diagram.

3. $\angle 3$ is also supplementary to $\angle 2$. Find the measure of $\angle 3$ and label the diagram.

4. From your work in Problems 1–3, make a conclusion about the measures of the vertical angles.

5. The diagram shows a light ray passing through a thin pane of glass. The ray hits the glass at $\angle 1$ to the surface. It then moves out the other side at $\angle 2$ to the surface so that $\angle 1$ and $\angle 2$ form vertical angles.

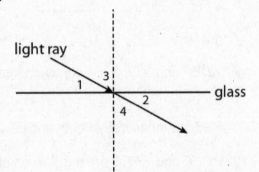

Write a two-column proof showing that if $\angle 1$ and $\angle 3$ are complementary, and $\angle 2$ and $\angle 4$ are complementary, then $m\angle 3 = m\angle 4$.

Statements	Reasons
1. $\angle 1$ and $\angle 2$ are vertical angles.	1. Given
2. a. _____	2. Vertical Angle Theorem
3. b. _____	3. Definition of Congruent Angles
4. $\angle 1$ and $\angle 3$ are complementary.	4. Given
5. c. _____	5. d. _____
6. $m\angle 1 + m\angle 3 = 90°$	6. Definition of Complementary Angles
7. e. _____	7. f. _____
8. g. _____	8. Substitution Property
9. $m\angle 3 = m\angle 4$	9. h. _____

LESSON 4-2

Transversals and Parallel Lines

Practice and Problem Solving: A/B

Find each angle measure.

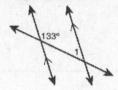

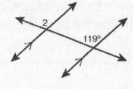

1. m∠1 _____

2. m∠2 _____

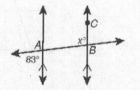

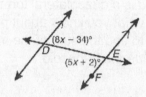

3. m∠ABC _____

4. m∠DEF _____

Complete the two-column proof to show that same-side exterior angles are supplementary.

5. **Given:** $p \parallel q$

   Prove: m∠1 + m∠3 = 180°

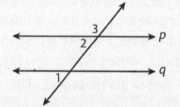

   Proof:

Statements	Reasons
1. $p \parallel q$	1. Given
2. a. _____	2. Lin. Pair Thm.
3. ∠1 ≅ ∠2	3. b. _____
4. c. _____	4. Def. of ≅ ∠
5. d. _____	5. e. _____

6. Ocean waves move in parallel lines toward the shore. The figure shows Sandy Beaches windsurfing across several waves. For this problem, think of Sandy's wake as a line. m∠1 ± (2x + 10)° and m∠2 = (4y − 30)°. Find *x* and *y*.

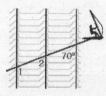

   x = _____

   y = _____

Transversals and Parallel Lines

Practice and Problem Solving: C

1. A *parallelogram* is a quadrilateral formed by two pairs of parallel lines. Use what you know about parallel lines and angle measures to find the sum of the measures of the four angles inside the parallelogram. Explain your answer.

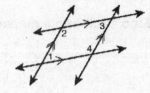

_____

_____

2. A *trapezoid* is a quadrilateral formed by one pair of parallel lines. Use what you know about parallel lines and angle measures to find the sum of the measures of the four angles inside the trapezoid.

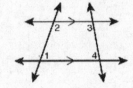

_____

3. A *trapezium* is a quadrilateral formed by four lines, no two of which are parallel. Find the sum of the measures of the four angles inside the trapezium. Write a two-column proof to justify your answer. (*Hint:* Draw $\overrightarrow{BE}$ parallel to $\overrightarrow{AD}$ and having *E* on $\overleftrightarrow{CD}$. Write *Construction* to justify this step.)

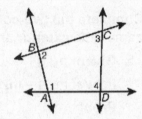

Given: The sum of the measures of the angles in a triangle is 180°.

Prove: m∠1 + m∠2 + m∠3 + m∠4 = _____

_____

_____

_____

_____

_____

_____

_____

_____

_____

Name _____ Date _____ Class_____

LESSON 4-3

Proving Lines Are Parallel

Practice and Problem Solving: A/B

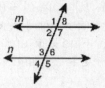

Use the figure for Problems 1–8. Tell whether lines *m* and *n* must be parallel from the given information. If they are, state your reasoning. (*Hint:* The angle measures may change for each problem, and the figure is for reference only.)

1. $\angle 7 \cong \angle 3$

2. $m\angle 3 = (15x + 22)°$, $m\angle 1 = (19x - 10)°$, $x = 8$

_____

_____

3. $\angle 7 \cong \angle 6$

4. $m\angle 2 = (5x + 3)°$, $m\angle 3 = (8x - 5)°$, $x = 14$

_____

_____

_____

_____

5. $m\angle 8 = (6x - 1)°$, $m\angle 4 = (5x + 3)°$, $x = 9$

6. $\angle 5 \cong \angle 7$

_____

_____

7. $\angle 1 \cong \angle 5$

8. $m\angle 6 = (x + 10)°$, $m\angle 2 = (x + 15)°$

_____

_____

9. Look at some of the printed letters in a textbook. The small horizontal and vertical segments attached to the ends of the letters are called *serifs*. Most of the letters in a textbook are in a serif typeface. The letters on this page do not have serifs, so these letters are in a sans-serif typeface. (*Sans* means "without" in French.) The figure shows a capital letter *A* with serifs. Use the given information to write a paragraph proof that the serif, segment $\overline{HI}$, is parallel to segment $\overline{JK}$.

Given: $\angle 1$ and $\angle 3$ are supplementary.

Prove: $\overline{HI} \parallel \overline{JK}$

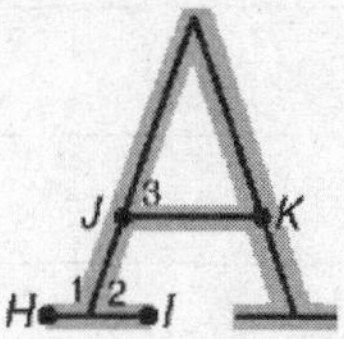

Name _____ Date _____ Class_____

Proving Lines Are Parallel

Practice and Problem Solving: C

1. $p \parallel q$, $m\angle 1 = (6x + y - 4)°$, $m\angle 2 =$
   $(x - 9y + 1)°$, $m\angle 3 = (11x + 2)°$
   Find x, y, and the measures of
   $\angle 1$, $\angle 2$, and $\angle 3$.

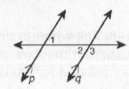

_____

2. A definition of parallel lines is "two coplanar lines that never intersect."
   Imagine railroad tracks or the strings on a guitar. Another way to think
   about parallel lines is that they extend in exactly the same direction.
   Or to say it more mathematically, if a third line intersects one line in a
   right angle and intersects a second line in a right angle, then the first
   and second lines are parallel. Use this last definition as the final step in
   a paragraph proof of the following.

   Given: The sum of the angle measures in any
   triangle is 180°; $\angle 1 \cong \angle 2$

   Prove: $\overleftrightarrow{AB}$ and $\overleftrightarrow{CD}$ are parallel lines.

   (*Hint*: First draw line $\overleftrightarrow{AE}$ so it forms a 90° angle with $\overleftrightarrow{AB}$.
   This step can be justified by the Protractor Postulate.
   On the figure, label the intersection of $\overleftrightarrow{AE}$ and $\overleftrightarrow{CD}$ point F.)

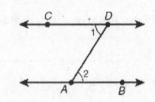

_____

_____

_____

_____

_____

_____

_____

3. $s \parallel t$, $m\angle 1 = (3x - 6)°$, $m\angle 2 = (5x + 2y)°$,
   $m\angle 3 = (x + y + 6)°$; Find x, y, and the measures
   of $\angle 1$, $\angle 2$, and $\angle 3$.

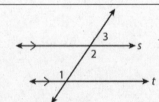

_____

_____

Name _____ Date _____ Class_____

LESSON
4-4

Perpendicular Lines
Practice and Problem Solving: A/B

For Problems 1–2, determine the unknown values.

1. Given: $\overleftrightarrow{AC}$ is the perpendicular bisector of $\overline{GH}$.

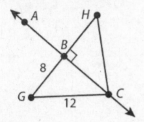

2. Given: $\overleftrightarrow{CD}$ is the perpendicular bisector of $\overline{PR}$.

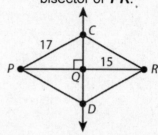

GH = _____

CH = _____

CR = _____

PQ = _____

Complete the two-column proof.

3. **Given:** $m \perp n$

   Prove: $\angle 1$ and $\angle 2$ are a linear pair of congruent angles.

   Proof:

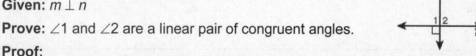

Statements	Reasons
1. a. _____	1. Given
2. b. _____	2. Def. of $\perp$
3. $\angle 1 \cong \angle 2$	3. c. _____
4. $m\angle 1 + m\angle 2 = 180°$	4. Add. Prop. of $=$
5. d. _____	5. Def. of linear pair

4. The Four Corners National Monument is at the intersection of the borders of Arizona, Colorado, New Mexico, and Utah. It is called the four corners because the intersecting borders are perpendicular. If you were to lie down on the intersection, you could be in four states at the same time—the only place in the United States where this is possible. The figure shows the Colorado–Utah border extending north in a straight line until it intersects the Wyoming border at a right angle. Explain why the Colorado–Wyoming border must be parallel to the Colorado–New Mexico border.

_____

_____

_____

LESSON 4-4

Perpendicular Lines

Practice and Problem Solving: C

1. Draw a segment a little more than half the width of this page. Label this segment with length x, then use a compass and straightedge to construct a segment that has length $\frac{5}{4}x$.

2. Among segments $\overline{BA}$, $\overline{BC}$, $\overline{BD}$, and $\overline{BE}$, which is the shortest segment in the figure? Name the second-shortest segment. Explain your answers.

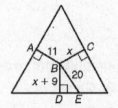

_____

_____

_____

_____

3. Use a straightedge to draw a triangle. Construct the perpendicular bisector of each side of the triangle, and extend the bisectors into the interior of the triangle. Mark the point of intersection of the three bisectors. This is the *circumcenter* of the triangle. Use your compass to compare the distance from the circumcenter to each vertex of the triangle. What is remarkable about the distances?

_____

Now construct a circle completely around the triangle through all three vertices with your compass. You have *circumscribed* a circle around a triangle.

4. An architect designs a triangular jogging track around a circular pond. Each side of the track just touches the pond. The circle is *inscribed* in the triangle. The center of the circle is called the *incenter* of the triangle. The diameter of the circle has length 41.

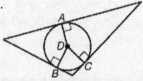

$DA = 8x + 2z - 1\frac{1}{2}$, $DB = 6x + y + 1$, $DC = 11y - 2z + 2$.

Find x, y, and z.

Name _____ Date _____ Class_____

Equations of Parallel and Perpendicular Lines
Practice and Problem Solving: A/B

Find the rise and the run between the marked points on each graph. Then find the slope of the line.

1.

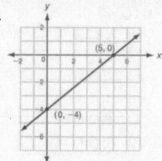

rise = _____ run = _____

slope = _____

2.

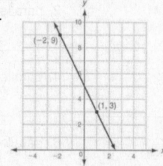

rise = _____ run = _____

slope = _____

3.

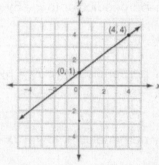

rise = _____ run = _____

slope = _____

Write an equation parallel to the given line through the given point.

4. parallel to $y = 9x + 4$
through (2, 7)

_____

5. parallel to $y = 4x - 6$
through (6, −3)

_____

6. parallel to $y = \frac{2}{3}x + 6$

through (−3, 6)

_____

7. parallel to $y = -\frac{1}{4}x - 12$

through (12, 10)

_____

Write an equation perpendicular to the given line through the given point.

8. perpendicular to $y = \frac{1}{4}x + 3$

through (4, 1)

_____

9. perpendicular to $y = -\frac{1}{3}x - 6$

through (−2, 8)

_____

10. perpendicular to $y = -6x - 9$
through (6, 10)

_____

11. perpendicular to $y = 5x + 14$
through (5, −3)

_____

LESSON
4-5

Equations of Parallel and Perpendicular Lines

Practice and Problem Solving: C

Write the equation of the line that is parallel or perpendicular to the graph of the given equation and that passes through the given point.

1. perpendicular to $x - 6y = 2$; (2, 4)

   _____

2. parallel to $y = x$; (7, –2)

   _____

3. perpendicular to $2x + 5y = -3$; (2, –3)

   _____

4. parallel to $5x + y = 2$; (2, 3)

   _____

5. perpendicular to $y = 3x - 2$; (6, –1)

   _____

6. parallel to $9x + 3y = 8$; (–1, –4)

   _____

For Problems 7–8, write the equation of the line that passes through (2, 7) and is perpendicular to the given line.

7. $y = -5$

   _____

8. $x = -5$

   _____

9. A line that passes through the points (2, 1) and (k, 5) is perpendicular to the line $y = 3x - 9$. Find the value of k.

   _____

10. The graphs of the equations $2x + 5y = 3$ and $2x + 5y = 7$ are parallel lines. Find the equation of the line that is parallel to both lines and lies midway between them.

    _____

11. A line on the coordinate plane passes through the points (7, –5) and (3, 11). A line that is perpendicular to the first line passes through the points (–3, –9) and (5, n). Find the value of n.

    _____

12. A line that passes through the points (2, –3) and (b, 7) is parallel to the line $y = -2x + 17$. Find the value of b.

    _____

13. The lines $x = 0$, $y = 2x - 5$, and $y = mx + 9$ form a right triangle. Find two possible values of m.

    _____

LESSON 5-1

Exploring What Makes Triangles Congruent

Practice and Problem Solving: A/B

$\triangle XYZ \cong \triangle NPQ$. **Identify the congruent corresponding parts.**

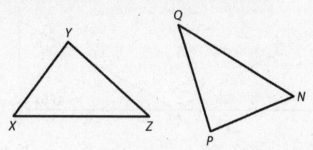

1. $\angle Z \cong$ _____

2. $\overline{YZ} \cong$ _____

3. $\angle P \cong$ _____

4. $\angle X \cong$ _____

5. $\overline{NQ} \cong$ _____

6. $\overline{PN} \cong$ _____

$\triangle LMN \cong \triangle CBA$. **Find each value.**

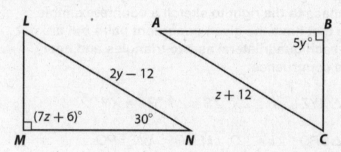

7. $z =$ _____

8. $y =$ _____

9. $m\angle L =$ _____

10. $LN =$ _____

11. $m\angle C =$ _____

12. $AC =$ _____

$\triangle QRS \cong \triangle JKL$.

13. Mark all the congruent corresponding parts of the two triangles.

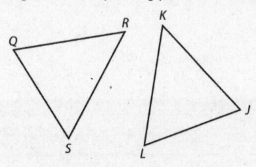

LESSON
5-1

Exploring What Makes Triangles Congruent

Practice and Problem Solving: C

$\triangle ABC \cong \triangle EDC$. $BD = 24$. Find each value.

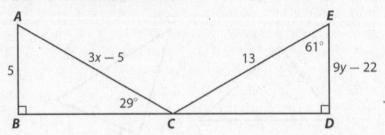

1. $m\angle A =$ _____

2. $BC =$ _____

3. $m\angle DCE =$ _____

4. $ED =$ _____

5. $x =$ _____

6. $y =$ _____

For each question below, two figures are named, and pairs of
congruent parts of the figures are given. Write $\cong$ in the blank if the
figures are definitely congruent. If there is not enough information,
write? and use the space to the right to sketch a counterexample
showing two figures that have the given congruent pairs but are not
congruent. Think of each quadrilateral as two triangles and apply
principles of triangle congruence.

7. $\triangle RST$ _____ $\triangle XYZ$: $\angle R \cong \angle X$; $\angle S \cong \angle Y$; $\overline{RS} \cong \overline{XY}$

8. $\triangle LMN$ _____ $\triangle OPQ$: $\angle L \cong \angle O$; $\overline{LM} \cong \overline{OP}$; $\overline{MN} \cong \overline{PQ}$

9. $ABCD$ _____ $EFGH$: $m\angle A = m\angle E = 90°$;

   $m\angle B = m\angle F = 90°$; $\overline{AD} \cong \overline{EH}$; $\overline{AB} \cong \overline{EF}$

10. $STUV$ _____ $WXYZ$: $m\angle S = m\angle W = 90°$;

    $m\angle U = m\angle Y = 90°$; $\overline{ST} \cong \overline{WX}$; $\overline{TU} \cong \overline{XY}$

11. $JKLM$ _____ $NPQR$: $\angle J \cong \angle N$; $\angle K \cong \angle P$;

    $\angle L \cong \angle Q$; $\overline{KL} \cong \overline{PQ}$

12. $CDEF$ _____ $GHIJ$: $\angle C \cong \angle G$; $\angle D \cong \angle H$; $\angle E \cong \angle J$;

    $\overline{CD} \cong \overline{GH}$; $\overline{DE} \cong \overline{HI}$; $\overline{EF} \cong \overline{IJ}$

LESSON 5-2

ASA Triangle Congruence
Practice and Problem Solving: A/B

Apply ASA Triangle Congruence to answer Problems 1–3.

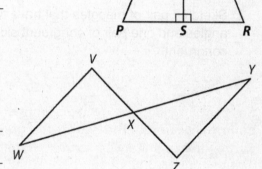

1. What additional information do you need in order to conclude that $\triangle PQS \cong \triangle RQS$? Explain your reasoning.

   _____

   _____

2. Point X is the midpoint of $\overline{VZ}$. Can you conclude that $\triangle VWX$ is congruent to $\triangle ZYX$? If so, explain your answer. If there is not enough information, explain what additional information is needed.

   _____

   _____

3. Angle D of $\triangle DEF$ is congruent to $\angle G$ of $\triangle GHJ$. Angle E is congruent to $\angle H$. Side DE is congruent to side HJ. Can you prove that the two triangles are congruent? Explain your answer.

   _____

   _____

For Problems 4 and 5, use the figure to the right.

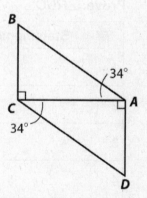

4. Complete the proof to prove that $\triangle ABC \cong \triangle CDA$.

Statements	Reasons
1. $\angle ACD \cong \angle$_____	1.
2.	2. Given
3.	3.
4. $\triangle ABC \cong \triangle CDA$	4.

5. Describe a sequence of two rigid motions that maps $\triangle ABC \cong \triangle CDA$.

   _____

   _____

LESSON 5-2

ASA Triangle Congruence

Practice and Problem Solving: C

Apply ASA Triangle Congruence to answer Problems 1–3.

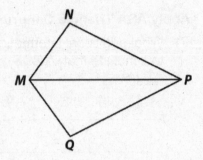

1. In the figure, *MP* bisects ∠*NMQ* and ∠*NPQ*. Explain how you know that *MN* = *MQ*.

   _____

   _____

2. Sketch a pair of triangles that have two pairs of congruent angles and one pair of congruent sides and are *not* congruent.

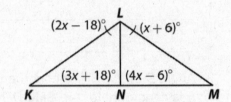

3. In the figure, *LN* bisects ∠*KLM*. Explain how you know that ∠*K* ≅ ∠*M*.

   _____

   _____

For Problem 4, use the figure to the right.

4. **Given:** ∠*PQU* ≅ ∠*TSU*; ∠*QUR* and ∠*SUV* are right angles; *QU* = *SU*
   Prove: ∠*RUQ* ≅ ∠*VUS*

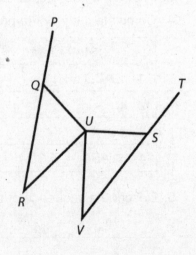

Statements	Reasons
1.	1.
2.	2.
3.	3.
4.	4.
5.	5.
6.	6.

LESSON 5-3 SAS Triangle Congruence

Practice and Problem Solving: A/B

Use principles of triangle congruence to answer Problems 1 and 2.

1. If you know the leg lengths of two right triangles, can you tell whether they are congruent? Explain your answer.

   _____

   _____

   _____

   _____

2. If two triangles have three pairs of congruent parts, will they always be congruent? Explain your answer.

   _____

   _____

   _____

   _____

For Problems 3 and 4, use the figure at the right.

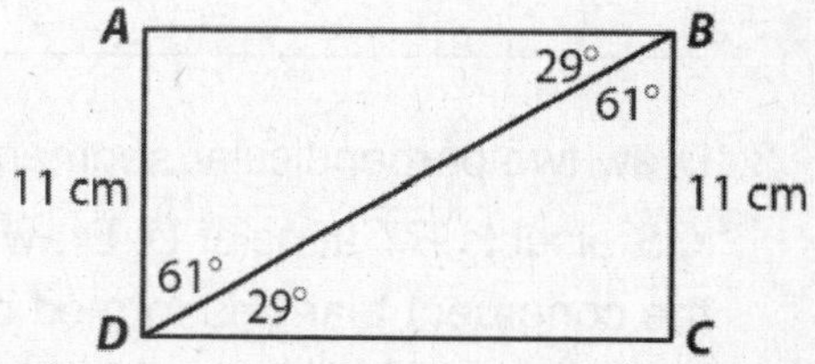

3. Explain how you know that △ABD ≅ △CBD.

   _____

   _____

   _____

4. Describe a sequence of two rigid motions that maps △ABD onto △CBD.

   _____

   _____

Use the figure at the right for the two-column proof.

5. The Hatfields and the McCoys are feuding over some land. Neither family will be satisfied unless the two triangular fields are exactly the same size. Point C is the midpoint of each of the intersecting segments. Write a two-column proof that will settle the dispute.

   Given: C is the midpoint of $\overline{AD}$ and $\overline{BE}$.

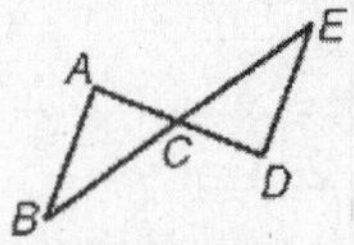

   Prove: △ABC ≅ △DEC

Statements	Reasons
1. C is the _____ of _____ and _____.	1. _____
2. AC = CD, _____ = _____	2. Definition of _____
3. $\overline{AC} \cong \overline{CD}$, _____ ≅ _____	3. Definition of _____
4. ∠ACB ≅ ∠_____	4. _____
5. _____ ≅ _____	5. _____

Name _____ Date _____ Class_____

SAS Triangle Congruence

Practice and Problem Solving: C

Use principles of triangle congruence for Problems 1–3.

1. In the figure, O is the center of the circle and $\angle DOE \cong \angle FOE$. Explain how you know that $\overline{DE} \cong \overline{EF}$.

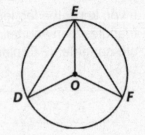

_____

_____

2. In the figure, M bisects $\overline{AC}$ and $\overline{BD}$. Also, $\angle BDA \cong \angle CAD$. Explain how you know that $\angle B \cong \angle C$.

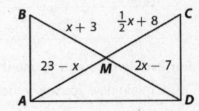

_____

_____

3. Draw two perpendicular segments, $\overline{QS}$ and $\overline{RT}$, such that $\overline{QS}$ bisects $\overline{RT}$ at point U. Draw figure QRST. Identify the congruent triangles formed by the figure and its diagonals, and tell how you know they are congruent.

_____

Use the figure to the right to do the two-column proof.

4. **Given:** $\overline{GH} \cong \overline{KL}$; $\overline{GH} \parallel \overline{KL}$; $\overline{FL} \cong \overline{JH}$

   Prove: $\angle FGH \cong \angle JKL$

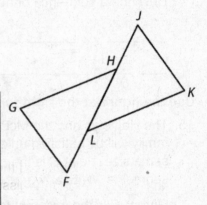

Statements	Reasons
1.	1.
2.	2.
3.	3.
4.	4.
5.	5.
6.	6.
7.	7.

Name _____ Date _____ Class _____

SSS Triangle Congruence
Practice and Problem Solving: A/B

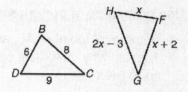

Use principles of congruence to answer Problems 1–3.

1. Show that $\triangle BCD$ is congruent to $\triangle FGH$ if $x = 6$.

   _____

   _____

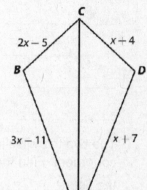

2. In the figure, $\overline{AB} \cong \overline{AD}$. Explain how you know that $\angle B \cong \angle D$.

   _____

   _____

   _____

3. In the figure, H is equidistant from the endpoints of line segment $\overline{GJ}$.
   Leon said that means that $\overleftrightarrow{HK}$ is the perpendicular bisector of $\overline{GJ}$.
   Was he right? Explain your reasoning.

   _____

   _____

   _____

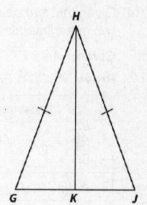

Use the figure at the right for the two-column proof.

4. Point O is the center of the circle. The chords $\overline{XY}$ and $\overline{ZY}$ are
   congruent. Fill in the missing statements and reasons to prove
   that $\angle X$ is congruent to $\angle Z$.

   Given: Circle O, $\overline{XY} \cong \overline{ZY}$

   Prove: $\angle X \cong \angle Z$

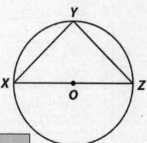

Statements	Reasons
1. $\overline{XY} \cong \overline{ZY}$	1.
2.	2.
3.	3. Reflexive property of congruence
4.	4.
5.	5.

Name _____ Date _____ Class _____

SSS Triangle Congruence

Practice and Problem Solving: C

Use principles of congruence for Problems 1–3.

1. J is the midpoint of AB, and $\overline{AK} \cong \overline{BK}$. Explain why $\triangle AKJ$ is congruent to $\triangle BKJ$.

   _____

   _____

   _____

   _____

2. Can a square be determined given only the length of a diagonal? Explain your answer.

   _____

   _____

   _____

   _____

3. The two triangles in the figure are congruent. Find the total area of the figure. _____ sq ft

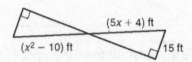

$(5x + 4)$ ft

$(x^2 - 10)$ ft   15 ft

Complete the two-column proof.

4. Given that two pairs of corresponding sides and three pairs of corresponding angles of two quadrilaterals are congruent, prove that the quadrilaterals are congruent.

   Given: $\overline{AB} \cong \overline{EF}$; $\angle B \cong \angle F$; $\overline{BC} \cong \overline{FG}$; $\angle C \cong \angle G$; $\angle D \cong \angle H$

   Prove: $ABCD \cong EFGH$

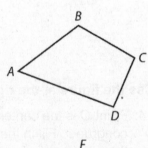
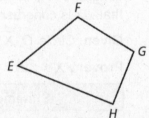

Statements	Reasons
1. $\overline{AB} \cong$ ____; $\angle B \cong$ ____; $\overline{BC} \cong$ ____	1.
2. $\triangle ABC \cong \triangle$ ____	2.
3. $\overline{AC} \cong \angle$ ____ and $\angle BCA \cong \angle$ ____	3.
4. $\angle C \cong \angle$ ____	4.
5. $m\angle C = m\angle BCA + m\angle$ ____ $m\angle G = m\angle$ ____ $+ m\angle$ ____ $m\angle ACD = m\angle$ ____	5. Angle addition
6. $\angle D \cong \angle$ ____	6.
7. $\triangle ACD \cong \triangle$ ____	7.
8. $\overline{CD} \cong \angle$ ____ and $\overline{AD} \cong \angle$ ____	8.
9.	9. All corresponding parts are congruent.

LESSON 6-1

Justifying Constructions

Practice and Problem Solving: A/B

The figure shows the construction line and arcs for drawing the angle bisector of ∠*ABC*.

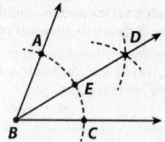

1. Name a point on the construction that is the same distance from *D* as *A* is.

   _____

2. Name a line segment that is congruent to $\overline{AB}$.

   _____

3. Suppose you drew segments $\overline{AD}$ and $\overline{DC}$. Which angle congruence theorem could you use to prove that △*BAD* ≅ △*BCD*? Explain your reasoning.

   _____

   _____

   _____

T is in the interior of ∠*PQR*. A student constructs $\overrightarrow{QT}$ so that it bisects ∠*PQR*. Find each of the following.

4. m∠*PQR* if m∠*RQT* = 11° _____

5. m∠*PQR* if m∠*RQT* = (5*x* − 7)° and m∠*PQT* = (4*x* + 6)° _____

6. m∠*TQR* if m∠*RQT* = (10*x* − 13)° and m∠*PQT* = (6*x* + 1)° _____

The figure shows △*FGH*, an isosceles triangle, constructed so that *GH* = *FH* and $\overline{GL}$ and $\overline{FL}$ are angle bisectors. Find each of the following quantities.

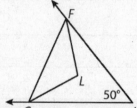

7. m∠*FGL* = _____

8. m∠*GFL* = _____

9. m∠*GLF* = _____

10. Joseph constructed two parallel lines and labeled the angles formed so that ∠3 and ∠7 were corresponding. He labeled m∠3 as (5*x* + 3)° and m∠7 as 68°. What is the value of *x*?

    _____

Justifying Constructions

Practice and Problem Solving: C

The diagram below shows how to construct one of the medians of the triangle. A median is a line segment between a vertex and the midpoint of the opposite side. Use the diagram to answer Problem 1.

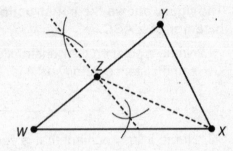

1. Identify any congruent segments and angles
   formed by the construction. Explain how you know
   they are congruent.

   _____

   _____

   _____

2. The figure at the right shows the result if the construction
   is completed and the midpoints are connected. Describe
   three pairs of congruent angles in the figure. Then identify
   the theorem that proves that they are congruent.

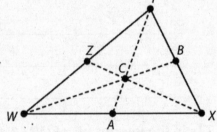

   _____

   _____

   _____

3. In an isosceles triangle, at least two of the angles are congruent. To
   construct isosceles triangle *DEH*, begin by drawing $\overrightarrow{DE}$ and $\overrightarrow{DF}$. If
   you copy ∠*FDE* and let the angle open in the same direction, the ray
   would be parallel to $\overrightarrow{DF}$. Instead, copy ∠*FDE* and draw $\overrightarrow{EG}$ so that
   the ray intersects $\overrightarrow{DF}$. Label the intersection point *H*. Measure $\overline{DH}$
   and $\overline{EH}$. What is remarkable about the lengths of these segments?

   _____

   _____

   _____

   _____

   _____

AAS Triangle Congruence

Practice and Problem Solving: A/B

1. Students in Mrs. Marquez's class are watching a film on the uses of geometry in architecture. The film projector casts the image on a flat screen as shown in the figure. The dotted line is the bisector of $\overline{AC}$. Can you use the AAS Theorem to prove that $\triangle ABD \cong \triangle CBD$? Explain why or why not.

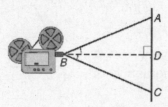

_____

_____

Write whether the AAS Congruence Theorem, the ASA Congruence Theorem, or neither can be used to prove the pair of triangles congruent.

2.

_____

3.

_____

4.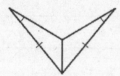

_____

5.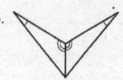

_____

Write a paragraph proof.

6. **Given:** ∠PQU ≅ ∠TSU
   ∠QUR and ∠SUR are right angles.
   Prove: △RUQ ≅ △RUS

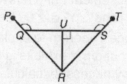

_____

_____

_____

Name _____ Date _____ Class _____

LESSON
6-2
AAS Triangle Congruence
Practice and Problem Solving: C

Explain the mistake in each proof in Problems 1–2. Then describe a correct way to prove that the triangles are congruent. Identify any additional information that is needed.

1. Given: $\overline{FD} \parallel \overline{BC}$, $\overline{AB} \parallel \overline{DE}$, and $\overline{AC} \cong \overline{FE}$

   Since $\overline{FD} \parallel \overline{BC}$, $\angle DFE \cong \angle ACB$ by the Alt. Int. ∠ Thm. Since $\overline{AB} \parallel \overline{DE}$, $\angle ABC \cong \angle EDF$ by the Alt. Int. ∠ Thm. Also, $\overline{AC} \cong \overline{FE}$ is given. Therefore, $\triangle ABC \cong \triangle EDF$ by AAS Congruence Theorem.

   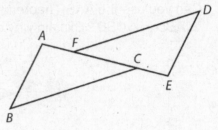

   Mistake: _____

   _____

2. Given: $\overline{AC} \cong \overline{CD}$; $\angle ACB$ and $\angle ECD$ are vertical angles.

   Since $\angle ACB$ and $\angle ECD$ are vertical angles, $\angle ACB \cong \angle ECD$ by the Vert. Angle Thm. $\overline{AC} \cong \overline{CD}$ is given. Since $\overline{AB} \parallel \overline{DE}$, $\angle ABC \cong \angle EDC$. Therefore, $\triangle ABC \cong \triangle DEC$ by AAS Congruence Theorem.

   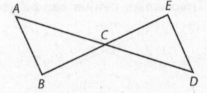

   Mistake: _____

   _____

Solve.

3. The grid shows the outlines of two exhibit areas at an amusement park. It is known that $\angle X \cong \angle P$ and $\angle Y \cong \angle Q$. Use the AAS Congruence Theorem to explain why the distance around the exhibits is the same. Make any necessary calculations.

   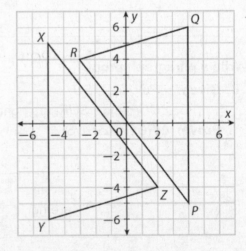

   _____

Original content Copyright © by Houghton Mifflin Harcourt. Additions and changes to the original content are the responsibility of the instructor.

44

LESSON 6-3

HL Triangle Congruence

Practice and Problem Solving: A/B

For Problems 1–3, use the HL Congruence Theorem to determine if the given triangles are congruent. For Problems 2 and 3, make sure the triangles are right triangles. Explain your answers.

1. △PQR and △STU

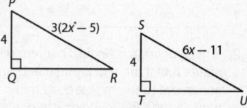

_____

_____

_____

2. A(–2, 2); B(4, –4); C(–2, –4); D(1, –1)

   △ACD and △BCD

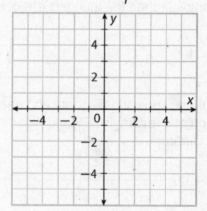

_____

_____

_____

3. A(0, 2); B(–4, 0); C(0, –3); D(–2, 1)

   △ACD and △BCD

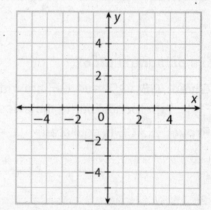

_____

_____

_____

4. Complete the proof.

   Given: isosceles triangle △PQS with $\overline{PQ} \cong \overline{PS}$

   and $\overline{PR} \perp \overline{QS}$

   Prove: △PQR ≅ △PSR

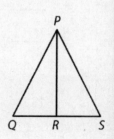

Statements	Reasons
1.	1. Given
2. ∠PRQ and ∠PRS are right angles.	2.
3.	3. Definition of right triangle
4.	4.
5.	5.

Name _____ Date _____ Class_____

LESSON 6-3

HL Triangle Congruence

Practice and Problem Solving: C

1. In what cases is knowing three parts (side lengths or angle measures) of a triangle not sufficient information to determine a specific triangle?

_____

_____

2. The Hypotenuse Angle Theorem (HA), similar to the HL Theorem, states that if the hypotenuse and one angle of a right triangle are congruent to the hypotenuse and corresponding angle of another right triangle then the triangles are congruent. Prove the HA Theorem.

_____

_____

3. If you know the diagonal and one side of a rectangle, can you draw a unique rectangle? Explain your answer and relate it to the HL Theorem.

_____

_____

_____

Write a paragraph proof.

4. **Given:** $\overline{GB}$, $\overline{GD}$, and $\overline{GF}$ are radii of the circle centered at G and are perpendicular to the sides of $\triangle ACE$.

   Prove: $\triangle ACE$ is equilateral.

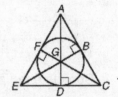

_____

_____

_____

_____

_____

Name _____ Date _____ Class _____

Interior and Exterior Angles

Practice and Problem Solving: A/B

Find the measure of each angle.

1.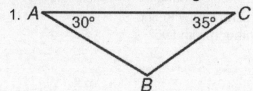

m∠B = _____°

2.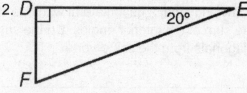

m∠F = _____°

3.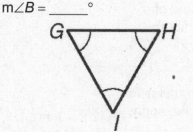

m∠G = _____°

4.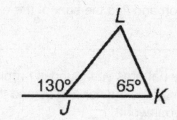

m∠L = _____°

5.

m∠P = _____°

6.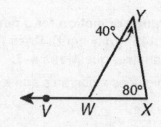

m∠VWY = _____°

Use your knowledge of angle relationships to answer questions 7–12.

7. The sum of the angle measures of a quadrilateral is _____°.

8. The acute angles of a _____ triangle are complementary.

9. The measure of an _____ angle of a triangle is equal to the sum of the measures of its remote interior angles.

10. The angle measures of a triangle are *a*, 3*a*, and 5*a*. Tell the measure of each angle. _____°, _____°, _____°

11. You know that one of the exterior angles of an isosceles triangle is

140°. The angle measures of the triangle could be _____°-_____°-

_____° or _____°-_____°-_____°.

Name _____ Date _____ Class_____

Interior and Exterior Angles

Practice and Problem Solving: C

Use your knowledge of interior and exterior angles to answer questions 1–3.

1. Draw and label a quadrilateral with one diagonal and show how to find the sum of the interior angles. Do the same for a pentagon with two diagonals from the same vertex.

   _____

2. Draw one exterior angle at each vertex of a quadrilateral and of a pentagon and find the sum of the exterior angles for each figure.

   _____

3. Use the patterns you found in problems 1 and 2 to write formulas for the sum of the interior angles and the exterior angles of a hexagon. Show your work.

   _____

The normal range of motion for a person's elbow is from 0° (fully extended) to 145° (fully bent). Draw figures and use your knowledge of angles to answer questions 4–8.

4. What angle does a person's arm form when it is fully bent at the

   elbow? _____°

5. Consider the triangle formed by Jared's elbow, the tips of his fingers when his arm is fully extended, and the tips of his fingers when his arm

   is fully bent. Name the angles of this triangle. _____°, _____°, _____°

6. After Ella broke her elbow, her maximum extension was 8°, and her maximum flexion was 136°. How many degrees of range of motion did

   she lose? _____°

7. With normal range of motion, a person can touch his or her shoulder with the fingers by bending the elbow and wrist. (Try it.) Given the measures below, use a protractor and ruler to draw and label a figure to illustrate this situation.

   shoulder to fingertips: 30 in.   elbow to wrist: 10 in.
   elbow to fingertips: 18 in.   flexion of wrist: 90°

8. Can Ella touch her shoulder with her fingers? Using the measurements in question 7 and Ella's flexion after breaking her arm, draw a figure and explain your answer.

   _____

LESSON 7-2

Isosceles and Equilateral Triangles

Practice and Problem Solving: A/B

For Problems 1–6, find each value.

1.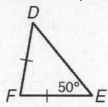

   m∠D = _____°

2.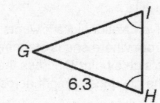

   GI = _____

3.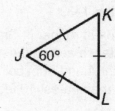

   m∠L = _____°

4.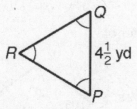

   RQ = _____

5.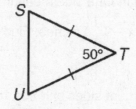

   m∠U = _____°

6.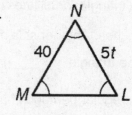

   t = _____

Use principles of isosceles and equilateral triangles to answer Problems 7–9.

7. Point *M* lies on side *JL* of triangle *JKL*. $\overline{KM}$ bisects $\overline{JL}$ and forms

   equilateral triangle *KLM*. What is the measure of ∠*J*? _____°

   Make a sketch and explain your answer. _____

   _____

   _____

8. Circle *B* and circle *C* are congruent. Point *A* is an
   intersection of the two circles. Write a paragraph
   proof to show that △*ABC* is equilateral.

   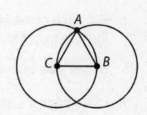

   _____

   _____

   _____

   _____

9. The Washington Monument is an *obelisk,* a tall, thin, four-sided
   monument that tapers to a pyramidal top. Each face of the pyramidal
   top of the Washington Monument is an isosceles triangle. The height
   of each triangle is 55.5 feet, and the base of each triangle measures
   34.4 feet. Find the length, to the nearest tenth of a foot, of one of the

   two congruent legs of the triangle. _____ ft

Isosceles and Equilateral Triangles

LESSON 7-2

Practice and Problem Solving: C

Use principles of isosceles and equilateral triangles to solve Problems 1–3.

1. A forest ranger in Grand Canyon National Park wants to find the distance across the canyon from where she is standing. From point *A* and from point *C*, she sights point *B* across the canyon. To the nearest 10 feet, find the distance straight across the canyon,

   from *D* to *B*. _____ ft

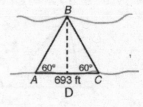

2. A triangle for billiards is equiangular. One side measures $(2x + 1)$ inches. Another side measures $(4x - 9\frac{1}{4})$ inches. Find the perimeter of the triangle. _____ in.

3. A regular pentagon has five congruent sides and five 108° angles, as shown in the figure. Find the angle measures: $x =$ _____; $y =$ _____;

   $z =$ _____

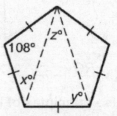

30 in.

David and Kellie have a piece of wood that is 30 inches square. They want to cut it to make a small tabletop in the shape of a regular octagon.

4. David says that a regular octagon is composed of eight isosceles triangles, so he suggests that they draw the four lines of symmetry and mark off the triangles. Draw a line to show where to make one of the cuts. Give the angle measures for the isosceles triangles.

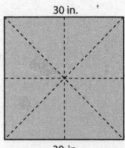

30 in.

   _____°, _____°, _____°

5. For each of the isosceles triangles, the ratio of the length of one of the congruent sides to the length of the base is 1.3. Tell the length

   of one side of the octagon to the nearest 0.1 inch. _____ in.

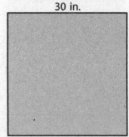

6. Kellie says it is possible to make a bigger regular octagon from the wood. Mark the figure to show how to make the biggest octagon possible. Explain your reasoning and tell

   the length of one side of the octagon. _____ in.

Quadratic Formula

$$x = \frac{-b \pm \sqrt{b^2 - 4ac}}{2a}$$

Name _____ Date _____ Class_____

Triangle Inequalities
Practice and Problem Solving: A/B

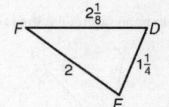

For Problems 1–3, name the angles or sides.

1. Write the angles of △*DEF* in order from smallest to largest.

   ∠ _____   ∠ _____   ∠ _____

2. Write the sides of △*GHI* in order from shortest to longest. .

   _____   _____   _____

3. The sides of triangle *XYZ* are given in order below from longest to shortest. Name the angles from largest to smallest.

   $\overline{XZ}$ $\overline{ZY}$ $\overline{YX}$

   ∠ _____   ∠ _____   ∠ _____

Use your knowledge of triangle inequalities to solve Problems 4–7.

4. Can three segments with lengths 8, 15, and 6 make a triangle? Explain

   your answer. _____

   _____

5. For an isosceles triangle with congruent sides of length *s*, what is the range of lengths for the base, *b*? What is the range of angle measures, *A*, for the angle opposite the base? Write the inequalities and explain

   your answers. _____

   _____

6. Aaron, Brandon, and Clara sit in class so that they are at the vertices of a triangle. It is 15 feet from Aaron to Brandon, and it is 8 feet from Brandon to Clara. Give the range of possible distances, *d*, from Aaron

   to Clara. _____

7. Renaldo plans to leave from Atlanta and fly into London (4281 miles). On the return, he will fly back from London to New York City (3470 miles) to visit his aunt. Then Renaldo heads back to Atlanta. Atlanta, New York City, and London do not lie on the same line. Find the range

   of the total distance Renaldo could travel on his trip. _____

   _____

LESSON 7-3

Triangle Inequalities

Practice and Problem Solving: C

In each figure, list the segments in order from longest to shortest.

1.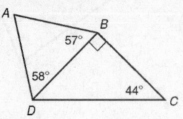

2.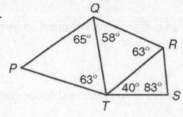

3.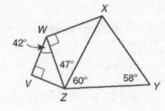

_____   _____   _____

Use principles of triangle inequalities to solve Problems 4 and 5.

4. In disc golf, a player tries to throw a disc into a metal basket target. Four disc golf targets on a course are shown at right.

   Which two targets are closest together? _____

   Which two targets are farthest apart? _____

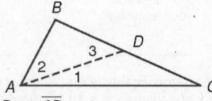

5. Name the shortest segment in the figure and explain your reasoning. Do not use a ruler. (*Note*: The figure may not be drawn to scale.)

_____

_____

_____

Describe how you could prove the theorem.

6. Unequal Sides Theorem
   Given: △ABC with BC > AB
   Prove: m∠ BAC > m∠C
   Plan for proof: Locate point D on $\overline{BC}$ such that BD = BA. Draw $\overline{AD}$.
   Explain why m∠BAC > m∠3, m∠3 > m∠C, and so m∠BAC > m∠C.

_____

_____

_____

_____

_____

_____

Perpendicular Bisectors of Triangles
Practice and Problem Solving: A/B

Use the figure for Problems 1–4.

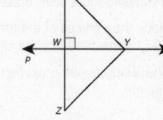

1. Given that line *p* is the perpendicular bisector of $\overline{XZ}$

   and *XY* = 15.5, find *ZY*. _____

2. Given that *XZ* = 38, *YX* = 27, and *YZ* = 27,

   find *ZW*. _____

3. Given that line *p* is the perpendicular bisector of $\overline{XZ}$,

   XY = 4*n*, and *YZ* = 14, find *n*. _____

4. Given that *XY* = *ZY*, *WX* = 6*x* − 1, and *XZ* = 10*x* + 16, find *ZW*. _____

Use the figure for Problems 5–6. $\overline{SV}$, $\overline{TV}$, **and** $\overline{UV}$ **are
perpendicular bisectors of the sides of** △*PQR*. **Find each length.**

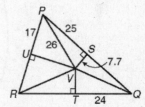

5. *RV* _____   6. *TR* _____

Find the circumcenter of the triangle with the given vertices.

7. *A*(0, 0), *B*(0, 5), *C*(5, 0)   8. *D*(0, 7), *E*(−3, 1), *F*(3, 1)

   (_____ , _____)   (_____ , _____)

Use the graph of △*ABC* **to complete Problems 9–15.**

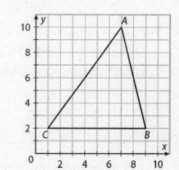

9. Draw a perpendicular bisector to $\overline{CB}$ on the graph.

10. Use the midpoint formula to determine the

    midpoint of $\overline{AC}$. _____

11. What is the slope of $\overline{AC}$? _____

12. What is slope of a line perpendicular to

    $\overline{AC}$? _____

13. Use the point-slope form to find the equation

    of the perpendicular bisector of $\overline{AC}$. _____

14. Draw the perpendicular bisector of $\overline{AC}$.

15. What is the point where the lines intersect called? _____

LESSON 8-1

Perpendicular Bisectors of Triangles

Practice and Problem Solving: C

1. Use construction tools to draw two different triangles within the circle below. Then draw perpendicular bisectors to each side of the triangles. Your drawing must have these properties:

   • Place the vertices of the triangles on the circle so that the triangles are circumscribed by the circle.

   • The circumcenter must be outside one triangle and inside the other triangle.

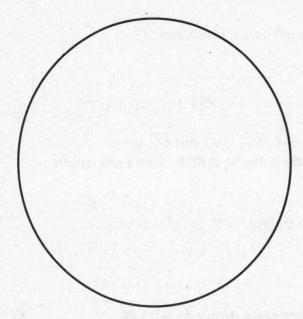

2. Compare the locations of the circumcenters of the triangles to the center of the circle. How does the length of each radius of a circle explain these locations?

   _____

   _____

3. A right triangle has a hypotenuse with length 17. What is the radius of

   the circle that can be circumscribed about this triangle? _____

4. $\overline{VS}$, $\overline{VT}$, and $\overline{VU}$ are perpendicular bisectors of the sides of △PQR. Find the circumference of the circle that can be circumscribed about this triangle.

   _____

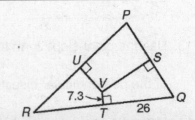

LESSON 8-2
Angle Bisectors of Triangles
Practice and Problem Solving: A/B

Use the figure for Problems 1–4.

1. Given that $FG = HG$ and $m\angle FEH = 55°$, find

   $m\angle GEH$. _____

2. Given that $\overline{EG}$ bisects $\angle FEH$ and $GF = \sqrt{2}$, find GH.

   _____

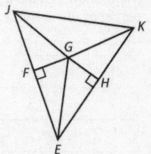

3. Given that $\angle FEG \cong \angle GEH$, $FG = 10z - 30$, and

   $HG = 7z + 6$, find FG. _____

4. Given that $GF = GH$, $m\angle GEF = \dfrac{8}{3}a°$, and $m\angle GEH = 24°$, find a. _____

Use the figure for Problems 5–9. $\overline{GJ}$ and $\overline{IJ}$ are angle
bisectors of $\triangle GHI$. **Find each measure.**

5. $m\angle JGK$ _____

6. $m\angle JIK$ _____

7. $m\angle KJI$ _____

8. the distance from J to $\overline{GH}$ _____

9. the distance from J to $\overline{IH}$ _____

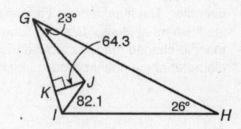

Solve.

10. Raleigh designs the interiors of cars. The
    triangular surface shown in the figure is
    molded into the driver's side door as an
    armrest. Raleigh thinks he can fit a cup
    holder into the triangle, but he'll have to
    put the largest possible circle into the
    triangle. Explain how Raleigh can do this.
    Sketch his design on the figure.

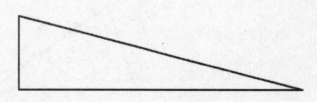

_____

_____

_____

_____

LESSON 8-2
Angle Bisectors of Triangles
Practice and Problem Solving: C

1. Draw a diagram and write a paragraph proof showing that the incenter and the circumcenter are the same point for an equilateral triangle. (*Hint:* Show that the angle bisector is the same line as the perpendicular bisector, or vice versa.)

    _____

    _____

    _____

    _____

    _____

    _____

2. Meteor Crater in northern Arizona was created by the impact of a relatively small meteor—about 80 feet in diameter. The figure shows the distances if the landowners at Meteor Crater built an equilateral triangle-shaped roadway around the crater. Find the diameter of the crater produced by the meteor.

    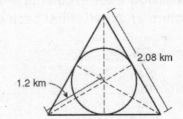

    _____

3. Construct angle bisectors from each vertex of the triangle in the figure, and mark the point where the bisectors intersect. Use this point as the center of a circle with a radius equal to the perpendicular distance from the center to one of the sides.

    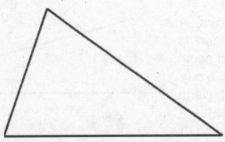

4. $\overline{KH}$ and $\overline{KJ}$ are angle bisectors of $\triangle HIJ$. Find the area of the circle that can be inscribed in this triangle.

    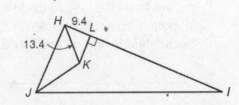

    _____

Name _____ Date _____ Class_____

LESSON 8-3

Medians and Altitudes of Triangles

Practice and Problem Solving: A/B

Use the figure for Problems 1–4. $GB = 12\frac{2}{3}$ and $CD = 10$.

Find each length.

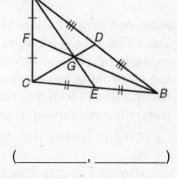

1. *FG* _____

2. *BF* _____

3. *GD* _____

4. *CG* _____

5. A triangular compass needle will turn most easily if it is attached to the compass face through its centroid. Find the coordinates of the centroid.

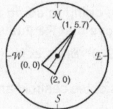

(_____ , _____)

Find the orthocenter of the triangle with the given vertices.

6. *X*(–5, 4), *Y*(2, –3), *Z*(1, 4)

(_____ , _____)

7. (0, –1), *B*(2, –3), *C*(4, –1)

(_____ , _____)

Use the figure for Problems 8 and 9. $\overline{HL}, \overline{IM}$, and $\overline{JK}$ are medians of $\triangle HIJ$. Round answers to the nearest tenth, if necessary.

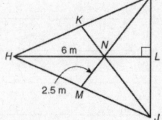

8. Find the area of the triangle. _____

9. What is *HJ*? _____

10. What is the perimeter? _____

11. Two medians of a triangle were cut apart at the centroid to make the four segments shown below. Use what you know about the Centroid Theorem to reconstruct the original triangle from the four segments shown. Measure the side lengths of your triangle to check that you constructed medians. (*Note:* There are many possible answers.)

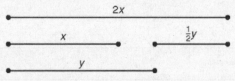
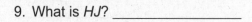

Medians and Altitudes of Triangles

Practice and Problem Solving: C

1. In a right triangle, what kind of line connects the orthocenter and the circumcenter?

_____

After noticing a pattern with several triangles, Regina declares to her class that in any triangle, the *x*-coordinate of the centroid is the average of the *x*-coordinates of the vertices, and the *y*-coordinate of the centroid is the average of the *y*-coordinates of the vertices. Regina used inductive reasoning to come to her conclusion. Use deductive reasoning to prove that Regina's conclusion is correct.

2. **Given:** $\triangle ABC$ with $A(0, 0)$, $B(2b, 2c)$, $C(2a, 0)$

   Prove: The coordinates of the centroid are $\left(\dfrac{2a + 2b}{3}, \dfrac{2c}{3}\right)$.

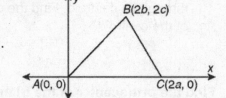

_____

_____

_____

_____

_____

_____

_____

_____

_____

_____

_____

_____

_____

_____

_____

Midsegments of Triangles
LESSON 8-4
Practice and Problem Solving: A/B

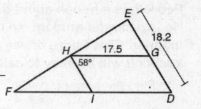

Use the figure for Problems 1–6. Find each measure.

1. *HI* _____

2. *DF* _____

3. *GE* _____

4. m∠*HIF* _____

5. m∠*HGD* _____

6. m∠*D* _____

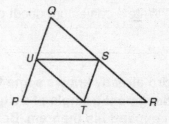

The Bermuda Triangle is a region in the Atlantic Ocean off the southeast coast of the United States. The triangle is bounded by Miami, Florida; San Juan, Puerto Rico; and Bermuda. In the figure, the dotted lines are midsegments.

	Dist. (mi)
Miami to San Juan	1038
Miami to Bermuda	1042
Bermuda to San Juan	965

7. Use the distances in the chart to find the perimeter of the Bermuda Triangle.

_____

8. Find the perimeter of the midsegment triangle within the Bermuda Triangle.

_____

9. How does the perimeter of the midsegment triangle compare to the perimeter of the Bermuda Triangle?

_____

Write a two-column proof that the perimeter of a midsegment triangle is half the perimeter of the triangle.

10. **Given:** $\overline{US}$, $\overline{ST}$, and $\overline{TU}$ are midsegments of $\triangle PQR$.

    Prove: The perimeter of $\triangle STU = \dfrac{1}{2}(PQ + QR + RP)$.

_____

_____

_____

_____

_____

_____

_____

_____

LESSON 8-4 Midsegments of Triangles

Practice and Problem Solving: C

Pedro has a hunch about the area of midsegment triangles. He is a careful student, so he investigates in a methodical manner. First Pedro draws a right triangle because he knows it will be easy to calculate the area.

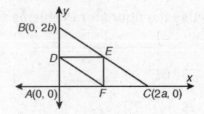

1. Find the area of △ABC. _____

2. Find the coordinates of the midpoints D, E, and F. _____

3. Pedro knows it will be easy to find the area of △EFD if ∠DEF is a right angle. Write a proof that ∠DEF ≅ ∠A.

4. Find the area of △EFD.   _____

5. Compare the areas of △ABC and △EFD.

   _____

6. Pedro has already shown that △EFD ≅ △ADF. Calculate the area of △ADF.   _____

7. Write a conjecture about congruent triangles and area.

   _____

Pedro already knows some things about the area of the midsegment triangle of a right triangle. But he thinks he can expand his theorem. Before he can get to that, however, he has to show another property of triangles and area.

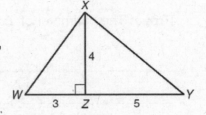

8. Find the area of △WXY, △WXZ, and △YXZ.

   _____

9. Compare the total of the areas of △WXZ and △YXZ to the area of △WXY.

   _____

   _____

10. Write a conjecture about the areas of triangles within a larger triangle.

   _____

   _____

Name _____ Date _____ Class_____

Properties of Parallelograms
Practice and Problem Solving: A/B

PQRS is a parallelogram. Find each measure.

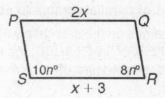

1. *RS* _____

2. m∠*S* _____

3. m∠*R* _____

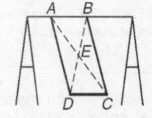

The figure shows a swing blown to one side by a breeze. As long as the seat of the swing is parallel to the top bar, the swing makes a parallelogram. In

$\square$ *ABCD*, *DC* = 2 ft, *BE* = $4\frac{1}{2}$ ft, and m∠*BAD* = 75°.

Find each measure.

4. *AB* _____   5. *ED* _____   6. *BD* _____

7. m∠*ABC* _____   8. m∠*BCD* _____   9. m∠*ADC* _____

Three vertices of $\square$ *GHIJ* are *G*(0, 0), *H*(2, 3), and *J*(6, 1). Use the grid to the right to complete Problems 10–16.

10. Plot vertices *G*, *H*, and *J* on the coordinate plane.

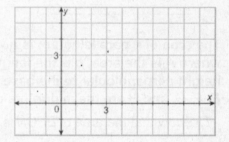

11. Find the rise (difference in the *y*-coordinates) from

   G to *H*. _____

12. Find the run (difference in the *x*-coordinates) from

   G to *H*. _____

13. Using your answers from Problems 11 and 12, add the rise to the
    y-coordinate of vertex *J* and add the run to the *x*-coordinate of vertex *J*.
    The coordinates of vertex *I* are (_____, _____).

14. Plot vertex *I*. Connect the points to draw $\square$ *GHIJ*.

15. Check your answer by finding the slopes of $\overline{IH}$ and $\overline{JG}$.

   slope of $\overline{IH}$ = _____   slope of $\overline{JG}$ = _____

16. What do the slopes tell you about $\overline{IH}$ and $\overline{JG}$? _____

   _____

| LESSON 9-1 | # Properties of Parallelograms |

Practice and Problem Solving: C

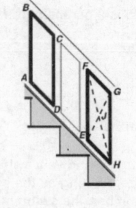

Use properties of parallelograms to solve Problems 1–3.

1. The wall frames on the staircase wall form parallelograms *ABCD* and *EFGH*. In □ *ABCD*, the measure of ∠*A* is three times the measure of ∠*B*. What are the measures

   of ∠*C* and ∠*D*? _____ ; _____

2. In □ *EFGH*, *FH* = 5*x* inches, *EG* = (2*x* + 4) inches, and *JG* = 8 inches. What is the length of *JH*?

   _____

3. The diagram shows a section of the support structure of a roller coaster. In □ *JKLM*, *JK* = (3*z* – 0.9) feet and

   LM = (*z* + 2.7) feet. Find *JK*. _____

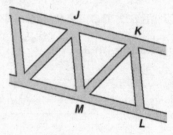

Find the range of possible diagonal lengths in a parallelogram with the given side lengths.

4. 3 and 12   5. *x* and 2*x*   6. *x* and *x*

_____   _____   _____

The area of a parallelogram is given by the formula A = bh, where A is the area, b is the length of a base, and h is the height perpendicular to the base. ABCD is a parallelogram. E, F, G, and H are the midpoints of the sides.

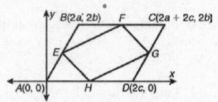

7. Show that the area of *EFGH* is half the area of *ABCD*.

8. Show that *EFGH* is a parallelogram.

Name _____ Date _____ Class_____

LESSON 9-2 **Conditions for Parallelograms**
Practice and Problem Solving: A/B

Determine whether each figure is a parallelogram for the given values of the variables. Explain your answers.

1. $x = 9$ and $y = 11$

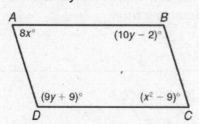

2. $a = 4.3$ and $b = 13$

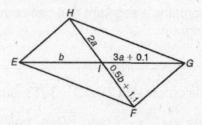

_____   _____

_____   _____

_____   _____

A quadrilateral has vertices $E(1, 1)$, $F(4, 5)$, $G(6, 6)$, and $H(3, 2)$. Complete Problems 3–6 to determine whether $EFGH$ is a parallelogram.

3. Plot the vertices and draw $EFGH$.

4. Use the Pythagorean Theorem to find the lengths of

   sides $\overline{EF}$ and $\overline{HG}$. $EF =$ _____ $HG =$ _____

5. Use the Slope Formula to find the slopes of sides $\overline{EF}$ and

   $\overline{GH}$. slope of $\overline{EF} =$ _____ slope of $\overline{HG} =$ _____

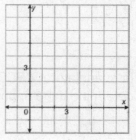

6. The answers to Problems 4 and 5 reveal important information about figure $EFGH$. State the theorem that uses the information found to prove that $EFGH$ is a parallelogram.

_____

_____

Use the given method to determine whether the quadrilateral with the given vertices is a parallelogram.

7. Find the slopes of all four sides: $J(-4, -1)$, $K(-7, -4)$, $L(2, -10)$, $M(5, -7)$.

_____

_____

8. Find the lengths of all four sides: $P(2, 2)$, $Q(1, -3)$, $R(-4, 2)$, $S(-3, 7)$.

_____

_____

Conditions for Parallelograms
Practice and Problem Solving: C

Use properties of parallelograms to solve Problems 1–4.

1. The graphs of $y = 2x$, $y = 2x - 5$, and $y = -x$ contain three sides of a quadrilateral in the coordinate plane. Give an equation of a line whose graph contains a segment that can complete the quadrilateral to form a parallelogram.

   _____

2. In parallelogram $ABCD$, $AC = 3\sqrt{13}$ and $BD = 5\sqrt{5}$. $\overline{AC}$ is contained in the line $y = \dfrac{3}{2}x - 2$, and $\overline{BD}$ is contained in the line $y = \dfrac{11}{2}x - 6$.

   If A and B are both in Quadrant I, find the vertices of $ABCD$.

   (*Hint:* All coordinates are integers.) _____

3. Find the slopes and lengths of one pair of opposite sides of quadrilateral $TUVW$. Is the figure a parallelogram with vertices $T\left(\dfrac{3}{2}, -2\right)$, $U\left(\dfrac{3}{2}, 4\right)$, $V\left(-\dfrac{1}{2}, 0\right)$, $W\left(-\dfrac{1}{2}, -6\right)$?

   _____

4. In quadrilateral $ABCD$, $\angle A \cong \angle B$ and $\angle C \cong \angle D$. Is it possible to determine if the opposite sides of the figure are parallel? Explain.

   _____

Write a two-column proof.

5. If the diagonals of a parallelogram are perpendicular and congruent, the figure is a square. (Diagonals intersect at point E.)

   Given: $ABCD$ is a parallelogram. $\overline{AC}$ and $\overline{BD}$ are perpendicular and congruent.

   Prove: $ABCD$ is a square.

Statements	Reasons
1.	1.
2.	2.
3.	3.
4.	4.
5.	5.
6.	6.
7.	7.

LESSON 9-3

Properties of Rectangles, Rhombuses, and Squares

Practice and Problem Solving: A/B

Tell whether each figure is a parallelogram, rectangle, rhombus, or square based on the information given. Use the most specific name possible.

1.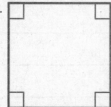

2.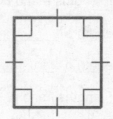

3.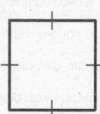

4.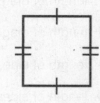

_____   _____   _____   _____

A modern artist's sculpture has rectangular faces. The face shown here is 9 feet long and 4 feet wide. Find each measure in simplest radical form. (*Hint:* Use the Pythagorean Theorem.)

5. $DC =$ _____

6. $AD =$ _____

7. $DB =$ _____

8. $AE =$ _____

VWXY is a rhombus. Find each measure.

9. $XY =$ _____

10. $m\angle YVW =$ _____

11. $m\angle VYX =$ _____

12. $m\angle XYZ =$ _____

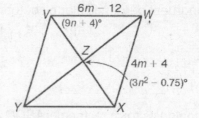

Write a paragraph proof.

13. **Given:** *ABCD* is a rectangle.
    Prove: $\angle EDC \cong \angle ECD$

_____

_____

_____

_____

_____

_____

Name _____ Date _____ Class_____

Properties of Rectangles, Rhombuses, and Squares

Practice and Problem Solving: C

For Problems 1–6, find the measures of the given figures.
For Problems 1–5, give your answers in simplest radical form.

1. length of diagonals of a rectangle with sides of lengths *a* and *b* _____

2. length of diagonals of a square with sides of length *s* _____

3. length of sides of a square with diagonals of length *d* _____

4. length of sides of a rhombus with diagonals of lengths *f* and *g* _____

5. length of a rectangle with width *w* and a diagonal of length 2*w* _____

6. measures of angles in the triangles formed by one diagonal of
   the rectangle in Problem 5.
   Explain how you found your answer. _____

   _____

   _____

Use the properties of special parallelograms to solve Problems 7 and 8.

7. The vertices of square *JKLM* are *J*(–2, 4), *K*(–3, –1), *L*(2, –2), and
   M(3, 3). Find each of the following to show that the diagonals of square
   JKLM are congruent perpendicular bisectors of each other.

   JL = _____   *KM* = _____

   slope of $\overline{JL}$ = _____   slope of $\overline{KM}$ = _____

   midpoint of $\overline{JL}$ = (_____, _____)   midpoint of $\overline{KM}$ = (_____, _____)

8. The soccer goalposts form rectangle *ABCD*. The
   distance between goalposts, *BC*, is 3 times the
   distance from the top of the goalpost to the ground.

   If the perimeter of *ABCD* is $21\frac{1}{3}$ yards, what is the

   length of diagonal $\overline{BD}$, to the nearest tenth of a foot? _____

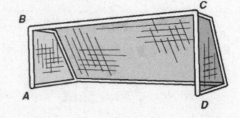

Write a paragraph proof for the statement.

9. If one pair of opposite angles of a quadrilateral are congruent and the
   diagonal bisects both angles, then the other diagonal bisects the other
   two angles.

   _____

   _____

   _____

Name _____ Date _____ Class_____

LESSON 9-4

Conditions for Rectangles, Rhombuses, and Squares
Practice and Problem Solving: A/B

Fill in the blanks to complete each theorem.

1. If one pair of consecutive sides of a parallelogram are congruent, then

   the parallelogram is a _____.

2. If the diagonals of a parallelogram are _____, then
   the parallelogram is a rhombus.

3. If the _____ of a parallelogram are congruent, then
   the parallelogram is a rectangle.

4. If one diagonal of a parallelogram bisects a pair of opposite angles,

   then the parallelogram is a _____.

5. If one angle of a parallelogram is a right angle, then the parallelogram

   is a _____.

Use the figure for Problems 6–7. Determine whether each conclusion is valid. If not, tell what additional information is needed to make it valid.

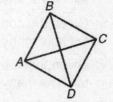

6. **Given:** $\overline{AC}$ and $\overline{BD}$ bisect each other. $\overline{AC} \cong \overline{BD}$

   Conclusion: *ABCD* is a square.

   _____

7. **Given:** $\overline{AC} \perp \overline{BD}, \overline{AB} \cong \overline{BC}$

   Conclusion: *ABCD* is a rhombus.

   _____

Complete Problems 8–11 to show that the conclusion is valid.

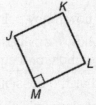

   Given: $\overline{JK} \cong \overline{ML}, \overline{JM} \cong \overline{KL}$; and $\overline{JK} \cong \overline{KL}$. $\angle M$ is a right angle.
   Conclusion: *JKLM* is a square.

8. Because $\overline{JK} \cong \overline{ML}$ and $\overline{JM} \cong \overline{KL}$, *JKLM* is a _____.

9. Because *JKLM* is a parallelogram and $\angle M$ is a right angle, *JKLM* is a

   _____.

10. Because *JKLM* is a parallelogram and $\overline{JK} \cong \overline{KL}$, *JKLM* is a _____.

11. Because *JKLM* is a _____ and a _____,
    JKLM is a square.

Conditions for Rectangles, Rhombuses, and Squares

LESSON 9-4

Practice and Problem Solving: C

1. Of a parallelogram, rectangle, rhombus, or square, name the two that can have a diagonal congruent to a side. Explain your reasoning.

   _____

   _____

   _____

2. Of the two quadrilaterals you named in Problem 1, with a diagonal congruent to a side, tell which one's diagonal length can be determined unambiguously given a side length (using only what you have learned in this geometry course so far). _____

3. If the congruent side and diagonal of the special quadrilateral from Problem 2 have length x, find the length of the other diagonal. _____

4. Give the measures of the interior angles of the special quadrilateral from Problem 2. _____

5. Given the coordinates of three vertices of a parallelogram, tell how many parallelograms can be formed. _____

6. Given the coordinates of three vertices of a rectangle, tell how many rectangles can be formed. _____

7. Given the coordinates of three vertices of a rhombus, tell how many rhombuses can be formed. _____

8. Given the coordinates of three vertices of a square, tell how many squares can be formed. _____

9. Given the coordinates of two vertices of a parallelogram, rectangle, or rhombus, tell how many of each can be formed. _____

10. Given the coordinates of two vertices of a square, tell how many squares can be formed. _____

11. Tell how many points are sufficient to determine a parallelogram. _____

12. Tell how many points are sufficient to determine a rectangle, a rhombus, or a square. _____

13. Find all the possible coordinates of the fourth vertex of a parallelogram with vertices (2, 3), (3, 0), and (4, 4). _____

14. Plot the three vertices given in Problem 13.
    Connect the vertices to make a triangle.
    Then plot the coordinates of all the possible
    fourth vertices. Connect these vertices.
    Name the relationship of the original triangle
    to the new figure you created.

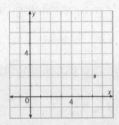

_____

LESSON 9-5

Properties and Conditions for Kites and Trapezoids

Practice and Problem Solving: A/B

In kite *ABCD*, m∠*BAC* = 35° and m∠*BCD* = 44°.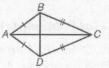
For Problems 1–3, find each measure.

1. m∠*ABD*

2. m∠*DCA*

3. m∠*ABC*

_____ _____ _____

4. Find the area of △*EFG*. _____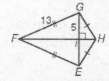

5. Find m∠*Z*.

6. *KM* = 7.5 and *NM* = 2.6. Find *LN*.

7. Find the value of *n* so that *PQRS* is isosceles.

_____

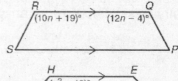

8. Find the values of *x* so that *EFGH* is isosceles.

_____

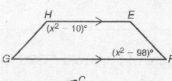

9. *BD* = 7*a* − 0.5 and *AC* = 5*a* + 2.3. Find the value of *a* so that *ABCD* is isosceles.

_____

10. *QS* = 8*z*², and *RT* = 6*z*² + 38. Find the values of *z* so that *QRST* is isosceles.

_____

Use the figure for Problems 11 and 12. The figure shows a ziggurat. A ziggurat is a stepped, flat-topped pyramid that was used as a temple by ancient peoples of Mesopotamia. The dashed lines show that a ziggurat has sides roughly in the shape of a trapezoid.

11. Each "step" in the ziggurat has equal height. Give the vocabulary term for $\overline{MN}$.

_____

12. The bottom of the ziggurat is 27.3 meters long, and the top of the ziggurat is 11.6 meters long. Find *MN*.

_____

LESSON
9-5

Properties and Conditions for Kites and Trapezoids

Practice and Problem Solving: C

Use the figure of kite *ABCD* for Problems 1–3.

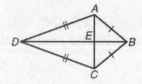

1. The figure shows kite *ABCD*. Find a formula for the area of a kite in terms of the diagonals *AC* and *BD*.

_____

2. Suppose you are given *BA*, *AC*, and *ED*. Tell whether it is possible to find the area of *ABCD*. Explain your answer.

_____

_____

_____

3. Suppose you are given *BA*, *DA*, and *BD*. Tell whether it is possible to find the area of *ABCD* (with what you have learned so far in this geometry class). Explain your answer.

_____

_____

Use the figure of trapezoid *PQRS* for Problem 4.

4. Write a paragraph proof.

   Given: $\overline{PQ} \parallel \overline{SR}$, $\overline{QU} \perp \overline{SR}$, $\overline{PT} \perp \overline{SR}$

   Prove: *PQUT* is a rectangle.

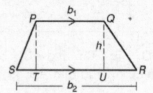

Use the figure of trapezoid *JKLM* for Problem 5.

5. Write a paragraph proof. **Given:** Isosceles trapezoid *JKLM*

   Prove: △*JNM* is isosceles.

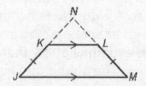

Slope and Parallel Lines

LESSON 10-1

Practice and Problem Solving: A/B

Line A contains the points (2, 6) and (4, 10). Line B contains the points (−2, 3) and (3, 13).

1. Are the lines parallel? Explain your reasoning.

    _____

    _____

Figure JKLM has as its vertices the points J(4, 4), K(2, 1), L(−3, 2), and M(−1, 5).

Find each slope.

2. $\overline{JK}$ 3. $\overline{KL}$ 4. $\overline{LM}$ 5. $\overline{MJ}$

    _____   _____   _____   _____

6. Is *JKLM* a parallelogram? Explain your reasoning.

    _____

    _____

For Problems 7–10, use the graph at the right.

7. Find the slope of line ℓ.

    _____

8. Explain how you found the slope.

    _____

    _____

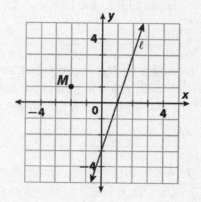

9. Line *m* is parallel to line ℓ and passes through point *M*.
   Find the slope of line *m*.

    _____

10. Find the equation of line *m*. Explain how you found the equation.

    _____

    _____

    _____

LESSON	**Slope and Parallel Lines**
10-1	

Practice and Problem Solving: C

Write the equation of the line that is parallel to the graph of the given equation and that passes through the given point.

1. $y = -6x + 4$; $(-2, 3)$ 2. $y = x$; $(7, -2)$

_____   _____

3. Quadrilateral $ABCD$ has vertices $A(-1, 5)$, $B(4, 0)$, $C(1, -5)$,
   and $D(-5, 1)$. Calculate the slopes of the sides, and then use
   your results to explain whether $ABCD$ is or is not a parallelogram.

_____

_____

_____

4. Find the equation of the line parallel to $2x + 5y = 3$ and
   $2x + 5y = 7$ that lies midway between them.

_____

5. A line that passes through the points $(2, -3)$ and $(b, 7)$
   is parallel to the line $y = -2x + 17$. Find the value of b.

_____

6. A line on the coordinate plane passes through the points $(-7, 8)$ and
   $(-7, 20)$. A line that is parallel to the first line passes through the points
   $(11, -4)$ and $(x, 9)$. Find the value of x.

_____

7. A line on the coordinate plane passes through the points $(-3, -7)$ and
   $(0, -5)$. A line that is parallel to the first line passes through the points
   $(6, 4)$ and $(-9, y)$. Find the value of y.

_____

8. Line L has the equation $ax + by = c$. Line M is parallel to Line L. What
   is the slope of Line M?

_____

LESSON 10-2 **Slope and Perpendicular Lines**

Practice and Problem Solving: A/B

Line A contains the points (−1, 5) and (1, −3). Line B contains the points (2, 3) and (−2, 2).

1. Are the lines perpendicular? Explain your reasoning.

   _____

   _____

Figure WXYZ has as its vertices the points W(2, 7), X(5, 6), Y(5, −4), and Z(−1, −2).

Find each slope.

2. $\overline{WX}$ 3. $\overline{XY}$ 4. $\overline{YZ}$ 5. $\overline{ZW}$

   _____   _____   _____   _____

6. Is Figure WXYZ a rectangle? Explain your reasoning.

   _____

   _____

For Problems 7–10, use the graph at the right.

7. Find the slope of line ℓ.

   _____

8. Explain how you found the slope.

   _____

   _____

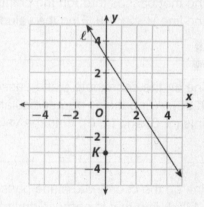

9. Line t is perpendicular to line ℓ and passes through point K.
   Find the slope of line t.

   _____

10. Find the equation of line t. Explain how you found the equation.

   _____

   _____

   _____

Slope and Perpendicular Lines
Practice and Problem Solving: C

Write the equation of the line that is perpendicular to the graph of the given equation and passes through the given point.

1. $x - 6y = 2$; (2, 4)

2. $y = -3x + 7$; (-3, 1)

_____

_____

For Problems 3–4, write the equation of the line that passes through the point (2, 7) and is perpendicular to the given line.

3. $y = -5$

4. $x = -5$

_____

_____

5. The sidewalks at a park can be modeled by the equations:
   $3(y + 1) = 2x$, $2y - 8 = -3x$, $2x + 3 = 3y$, and $-2(y - 12) = 3x$.
   Determine the slopes of the equations, and then use them to
   classify the quadrilateral bounded by the sidewalks.

   _____

   _____

6. A line that passes through the points (2, 1) and (k, 5) is perpendicular
   to the line $y = 3x - 9$. Find the value of k.

   _____

7. A line on the coordinate plane passes through the points (-3, 8) and
   (-9, 20). A line that is perpendicular to the first line passes through the
   points (5, 0) and (h, 6). Find the value of h.

   _____

8. A line on the coordinate plane passes through the points (7, -5) and
   (3, 11). A line that is perpendicular to the first line passes through the
   points (-3, -9) and (5, n). Find the value of n.

   _____

9. The lines $x = 0$, $y = 2x - 5$, and $y = mx + 9$ form a right triangle. Find
   two possible values of m.

   _____

Name _____ Date _____ Class_____

LESSON 10-3 **Coordinate Proof Using Distance with Segments and Triangles**
Practice and Problem Solving: A/B

Position an isosceles triangle with sides of 8 units, 5 units, and 5 units in the coordinate plane. Label the coordinates of each vertex. (*Hint:* Use the Pythagorean Theorem.)

1. Center the long side on the *x*-axis at the origin.

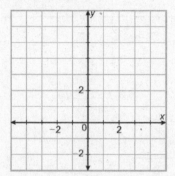

2. Center the long side on the *y*-axis at the origin.

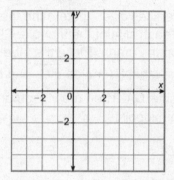

Complete Problems 3–5 to finish the proof.

Given: Triangle *ABC* is an isosceles triangle with vertices *A*(0, 0), *B*(8, 0), *C*(4, 10). Points *D, E, F* are the midpoints of triangle *ABC*.

Prove: Triangle *DEF* is an isosceles triangle.

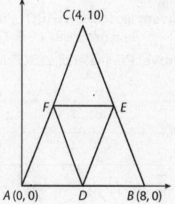

3. Use the midpoint formula to find the coordinates:

   D _____ *E* _____ *F* _____

4. Use the distance formula to show equal side lengths.

   DE = _____ *DF* = _____

5. Suppose, instead, that you want to use △*ABC* to prove the Midsegment Theorem, given that $\overline{FE}$ is a midsegment and $\overline{AB} \parallel \overline{FE}$. What other steps would you need in the

   coordinate proof? _____

   _____

LESSON 10-3

Coordinate Proof Using Distance with Segments and Triangles
Practice and Problem Solving: C

1. Position an isosceles triangle on the coordinate plane at the right so that you can use it for a coordinate proof. Place its base on the *x*-axis and draw it so that it is symmetric about the *y*-axis. Label the vertices $A(2a, 0)$, $B(0, 2b)$, and $C(-2a, 0)$.

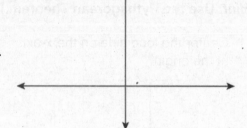

2. Using the vertices given, determine the midpoint of each side of the triangle. Plot the midpoints on the graph. Place the label D for side $\overline{AB}$, the label E for side $\overline{BC}$, and the label F for side $\overline{CA}$. Then draw segments to connect the midpoints.

   Midpoints: D _____ E _____ F _____

3. Use the graph you have constructed to write a coordinate proof.

   Given: Isosceles $\triangle ABC$ with $AB = BC$
   and midpoints D, E, F
   Prove: Perimeter of $\triangle DEF$ is one-half the perimeter of $\triangle ABC$.

   _____

   _____

   _____

4. One leg of a right triangle is 2.5 times the length of the other leg. Draw the triangle in the first quadrant of the coordinate plane with the legs along the axes and a vertex at the origin. Use only integer values for your coordinates and write each value as a multiple of *a*.

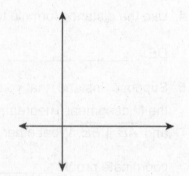

LESSON 10-4 **Coordinate Proof Using Distance with Quadrilaterals**

Practice and Problem Solving: A/B

Position a trapezoid with parallel sides of 4 units and 6 units in the coordinate plane. Label the coordinates of each vertex.

1. Center the long parallel side at the origin.

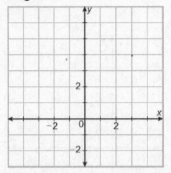

2. Center the long parallel side on the y-axis at the origin.

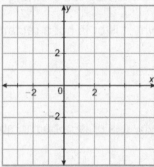

3. Describe the possible steps in a coordinate proof that would show that the figure you drew in Problem 1 is a trapezoid.

_____

_____

_____

Write a coordinate proof.

4. **Given:** Rectangle *ABCD* has vertices *A*(0, 4), *B*(6, 4), *C*(6, 0), and *D*(0, 0). *E* is the midpoint of $\overline{DC}$. *F* is the midpoint of $\overline{DA}$.

   Prove: The area of rectangle *DEGF* is one-fourth the area of rectangle *ABCD*.

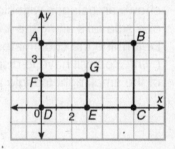

_____

_____

_____

_____

_____

_____

LESSON 10-4

Coordinate Proof Using Distance with Quadrilaterals

Practice and Problem Solving: C

1. A parallelogram has vertices $J(0, -4)$, $K(5, -1)$, $L(4, 4)$, and $M(-1, 1)$.
   Use a coordinate proof to decide whether it is a rectangle, a rhombus,
   or a square. It may be neither, or it may be more than one of these.

   a. Draw the parallelogram on the grid.

   b. Explain why it is or is not a rectangle.

   _____

   _____

   c. Explain why it is or is not a rhombus.

   _____

   _____

   d. Explain why it is or is not a square.

   _____

   _____

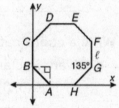

2. A stop sign is a regular octagon. A regular octagon has eight
   congruent sides and eight congruent 135° angles. The figure
   shows an octagon with side length ℓ in a coordinate plane so that
   one side falls along the *x*-axis and one side falls along the *y*-axis.
   Determine the coordinates of each vertex in terms of ℓ.
   (*Hint:* You will have to discover a relationship between the sides
   of the small right triangle at the origin.)

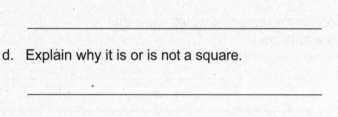

   _____

   _____

3. A "slow down" sign is a regular hexagon. A regular hexagon has
   six congruent sides and six congruent 120° angles. The ℓ figure
   shows a hexagon with side length ℓ in a coordinate plane so that
   one side falls along the *x*-axis and one vertex falls along the *y*-axis.
   Determine the coordinates of each vertex in terms of ℓ.

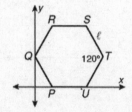

   _____

   _____

LESSON 10-5

Perimeter and Area on the Coordinate Plane

Practice and Problem Solving: A/B

Draw and classify each polygon with the given vertices. Find the perimeter and area of the polygon to the nearest tenth.

1. $A(-2, 3)$, $B(3, 1)$, $C(-2, -1)$, $D(-3, 1)$

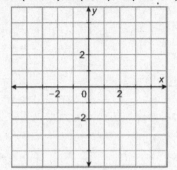

2. $P(-3, -4)$, $Q(3, -3)$, $R(3, -2)$, $S(-3, 2)$

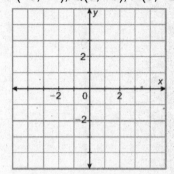

_____

3. $E(-4, 1)$, $F(-2, 3)$, $G(-2, -4)$

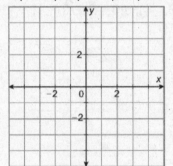

4. $T(1, -2)$, $U(4, 1)$, $V(2, 3)$, $W(-1, 0)$

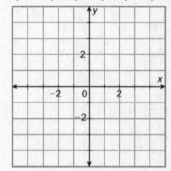

_____

Find the area and perimeter of each composite figure to the nearest tenth.

5.

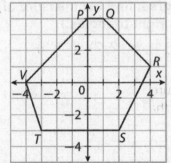

6.

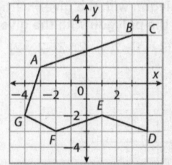

_____

LESSON 10-5

Perimeter and Area on the Coordinate Plane

Practice and Problem Solving: C

Draw each polygon with the given vertices. Find the perimeter and area of the polygon to the nearest tenth.

1. $A(0, 0)$, $B(2, 2)$, $C(-2, 0)$, $D(1, -2)$

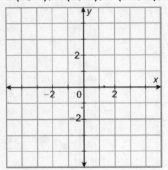

_____

2. $J(2, 4)$, $K(3, -4)$, $L(1, -2)$, $M(-1, -4)$

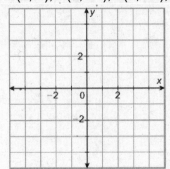

_____

3. $P(-3, 3)$, $Q(1, 2)$, $R(3, -3)$, $S(1, -3)$, $T(-2, -2)$

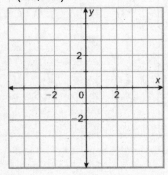

_____

4. $D(2, -1)$, $E(0, 0)$, $F(1, -2)$, $G(0, -4)$, $H(2, -3)$, $I(3, -4)$, $J(3, -2)$, $K(4, 1)$

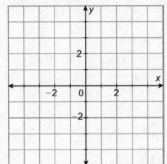

_____

Draw each polygon with the given vertices. To the nearest degree, find the measure of each angle in the polygon with the given vertices. (*Hint:* Form right triangles.)

5. $W(0, 0)$, $X(3, -1)$, $Y(1, -2)$, $Z(-2, -2)$

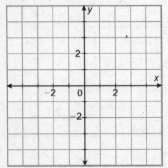

_____

_____

6. $F(3, 4)$, $G(1, 1)$, $H(-2, 2)$, $I(-3, 3)$

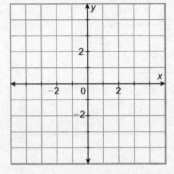

_____

_____

LESSON 11-1

Dilations

Practice and Problem Solving: A/B

For Problems 1 and 2, apply the dilation *D* to the polygon with the given vertices. Name the coordinates of the image points, and plot the pre-image and the image. Tell the scale factor.

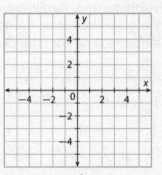

1. $D(x, y) \rightarrow (1.5x, 1.5y)$

   $G(1, -2), H(1, -4), J(4, -2)$

   $G'(\_\_\_\_, \_\_\_\_), H'(\_\_\_\_, \_\_\_\_); J'(\_\_\_\_, \_\_\_\_)$

   Scale factor: _____

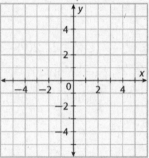

2. $D(x, y) \rightarrow \left(\dfrac{1}{3}x, \dfrac{1}{3}y\right)$

   $L(-3, 3), M(3, 6), N(3, -3)$

   $L'(\_\_\_\_, \_\_\_\_), M'(\_\_\_\_, \_\_\_\_), N'(\_\_\_\_, \_\_\_\_)$

   Scale factor: _____

For Problems 3–6, use your graphs for Problems 1 and 2.

3. If you drew lines $\overleftrightarrow{GG'}$, $\overleftrightarrow{HH'}$, and $\overleftrightarrow{JJ'}$, on the graph for Problem 1,

   where would the lines intersect? (____, ____) This point is called the

   _____ of _____.

4. If you drew lines $\overleftrightarrow{LL'}$, $\overleftrightarrow{MM'}$, and $\overleftrightarrow{NN'}$ on the graph for Problem 2,

   where would the lines intersect? (____, ____)

5. Fill in the lengths of the segments in Problem 1. Express each ratio as a decimal.

   $\dfrac{G'H'}{GH} = \dfrac{\Box}{\Box} = \_\_\_\_ \qquad \dfrac{J'G'}{JG} = \dfrac{\Box}{\Box} = \_\_\_\_$

6. Fill in the lengths of the segments in Problem 2. Express each ratio in radical form, if necessary, and then as a fraction in lowest terms.

   $\dfrac{L'M'}{LM} = \dfrac{\Box}{\Box} = \dfrac{\Box}{\Box} \qquad \dfrac{M'N'}{MN} = \dfrac{\Box}{\Box} = \dfrac{\Box}{\Box} \qquad \dfrac{N'L'}{NL} = \dfrac{\Box}{\Box} = \dfrac{\Box}{\Box}$

LESSON 11-1 Dilations

Practice and Problem Solving: C

For Problems 1–3, apply the dilation *D* to the polygon with the given vertices. Name the coordinates of the image points, and plot the preimage and the image.

1. $D(x, y) \rightarrow (0.75x, 0.75y)$

   $E(-4, 6)$, $F(-2, 2)$, $G(4, -2)$, $H(4, 4)$

   $E'(\_\_\_, \_\_\_)$, $F'(\_\_\_, \_\_\_)$, $G'(\_\_\_, \_\_\_)$, $H'(\_\_\_, \_\_\_)$

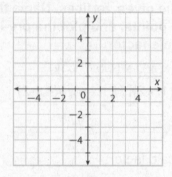

2. $D(x, y) \rightarrow (2(x + 2), 2(y - 3))$

   $J(-2, 2)$, $K(-4, 1)$, $L(1, 0)$

   $J'(\_\_\_, \_\_\_)$, $K'(\_\_\_, \_\_\_)$, $L'(\_\_\_, \_\_\_)$

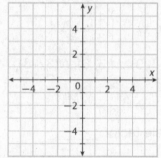

3. $D(x, y) \rightarrow \left(\frac{1}{3}(x - 1), \frac{1}{3}(y + 2)\right)$

   $X(-5, -5)$, $Y(-2, 4)$, $Z(4, 4)$

   $X'(\_\_\_, \_\_\_)$, $Y'(\_\_\_, \_\_\_)$, $Z'(\_\_\_, \_\_\_)$

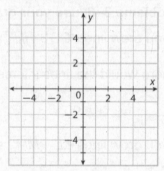

To solve Problems 4–7, refer to your graphs for Problems 1–3.

4. In Problem 1, find the lengths of $\overline{H'G'}$ and $\overline{HG}$.

   $H'G' = $ _____. $HG = $ _____. Write the ratio $\dfrac{H'G'}{HG}$ as a

   fraction in lowest terms. _____ What is the scale

   factor? _____

5. In Problem 2, find $J'L'$ and JL in radical form. Write their ratio and

   simplify. _____ In Problem 3, find the ratio of $X'Y'$ and XY and

   simplify. _____

6. In Problem 1, if you drew $\overleftrightarrow{EE'}$, $\overleftrightarrow{FF'}$, $\overleftrightarrow{GG'}$, and $\overleftrightarrow{HH'}$, where would

   they intersect? _____ This is the center of dilation.

7. Find the center of dilation for Problem 2. _____

Name _____ Date _____ Class_____

LESSON
11-2

Proving Figures are Similar Using Transformations

Practice and Problem Solving: A/B

**For Problems 1–4, prove that the figures are similar by describing
a series of transformations that maps one figure to the other.**

1. Circle *A* has a radius of 4 and a center at (3, 0). Circle *B*
   has a radius of 3 and a center at (2, 3). What series of transformations
   maps Circle *A* to Circle *B*, proving that they are similar?

   _____

   _____

2. *A*(1, 1), *B*(2, 4), *C*(3, 9)

   D(1.5, 1.5), *E*(3, 6), *F*(4.5, 13.5)

   _____

3. *GHIJ* and *KLMN*

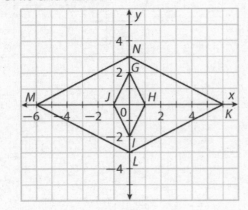

4. *A*(–4, 4), *B*(0, 4), *C*(0, 0), *D*(–2, –2), *E*(–4, 0)

   P(–3, 3), *Q*(–1, 3), *R*(–1, 1), *S*(–2, 0), *T*(–3, 1)

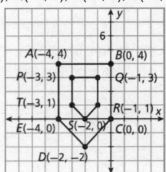

_____   _____

**Tell whether the following pairs of figures are always (A),
sometimes (S), or never (N) similar.**

5. Two quadrilaterals with congruent corresponding angles _____

6. Two isosceles trapezoids with proportional corresponding sides _____

7. Two regular pentagons _____

8. Two quadrilaterals with proportional corresponding sides _____

9. A parallelogram and a trapezoid _____

10. Two rhombuses with congruent corresponding angles _____

Original content Copyright © by Houghton Mifflin Harcourt. Additions and changes to the original content are the responsibility of the instructor.

83

Name _____ Date _____ Class_____

Proving Figures are Similar Using Transformations
Practice and Problem Solving: C

For Problems 1–4, tell what series of transformations will map the first figure to the second. If the figures are not similar, write *None*, and explain why they are not similar.

1. $A(-3, -2)$, $B(-2, 1)$, $C(2, 2)$ _____

   $D(-6, -4)$, $E(-4, 3)$, $F(4, 4)$ _____

2. $O(-2, -1)$, $P(-2, 1)$, $Q(0, 2)$, $R(2, 1)$,
   $S(2, -1)$, $T(0, -2)$

   $U(-2, 4)$, $V(2, 4)$, $W(4, 0)$, $X(2, -4)$,
   $Y(-2, -4)$, $Z(-4, 0)$

   _____

   _____

   _____

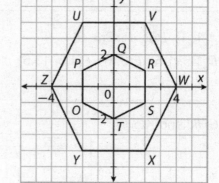

3. $P(2, 2)$, $Q(2, 4)$, $R(4, 6)$, $S(6, 6)$
   $T(1, -1)$, $U(1, -2)$, $V(2, -3)$, $W(3, -3)$

   _____

   _____

   _____

4. Circle A with center $(-1, -3)$ and radius 8
   Circle B with center $(-5, -3)$ and radius 2

   _____

   _____

Determine whether or not these triangles are similar by finding the ratios of the lengths of corresponding sides.

5. $A(-6, 5)$, $B(-4.5, 2)$, $C(0, 5)$ and $D(1, 2)$, $E(2, 4)$, $F(5, 2)$ _____

6. $A(1, 1)$, $B(1, 4)$, $C(6, 1)$ and $D(-4, -4)$, $E(-4, 0)$, $F(3, -4)$ _____

7. $A(-5, -1)$, $B(-2, 5)$, $C(1, -1)$ and $D(2, -4)$, $E(3, -2)$, $F(4, -4)$ _____

LESSON 11-3

Corresponding Parts of Similar Figures

Practice and Problem Solving: A/B

For Problems 1–3, apply properties of similar figures.

1. Devon says that triangles *TUV* and *XYZ* are similar because $\dfrac{TU}{XY} = \dfrac{UV}{YZ} = \dfrac{XZ}{TV}$. What is wrong with his reasoning?

   _____

2. Triangles *CDE* and *FGH* are similar. Write three proportions relating the triangles' side lengths, and three statements about their angle measures.

   _____

3. Are all rhombuses similar? Explain your answer.

   _____

Use the diagram for Problems 4 and 5.

4. In the diagram of the tandem bike, $\overline{AE} \parallel \overline{BD}$. Explain why $\triangle CBD \sim \triangle CAE$.

   _____

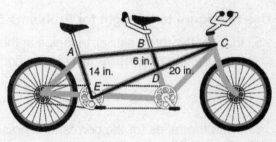

5. Find *CE* to the nearest tenth. Show your work.

   _____

For Problems 6 and 7, show that the figures are similar by using a ruler to find the center of dilation. Name the center point.

6. (_____, _____)   7. (_____, _____)

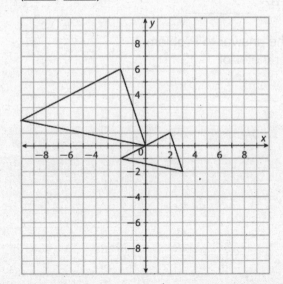

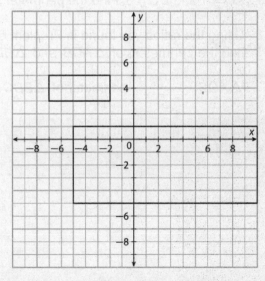

LESSON 11-3

Corresponding Parts of Similar Figures

Practice and Problem Solving: C

Use principles of similarity to solve Problems 1–4.

1. Triangles *CDE* and *FGH* are similar. Write six different proportions relating the side lengths of the triangles, and three statements about their angle measures.

2. Study the proportions you wrote for Problem 1. Pick out two different proportions that relate the same four side lengths. Using *w, x, y,* and *z* to stand for the four side lengths, write algebraic equations to show why the two proportions are equivalent. Explain your reasoning.

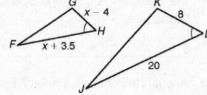

3. Find the value of *x* that makes $\triangle FGH \sim \triangle JKL$.

   _____

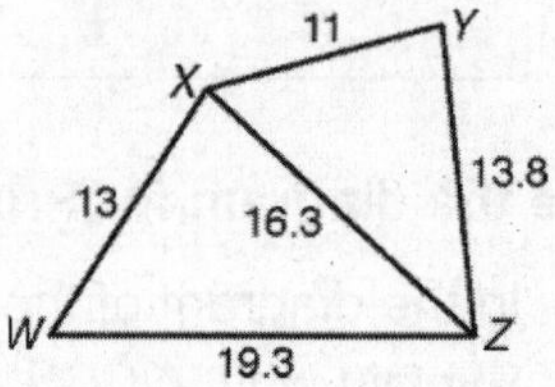

4. Is $\triangle WXZ \sim \triangle XYZ$? Explain.

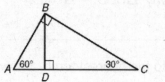

   _____

Use the figure to the right for Problems 5–8.

5. Identify the three similar triangles in the figure. Be sure to name the vertices in the correct order.

   $\triangle ABC \sim \triangle$ _____ $\sim \triangle$ _____

6. Write the ratios for the corresponding sides of each pair of similar triangles. (Note: The hypotenuse of a 30-60-90 triangle is twice as long as the shorter leg.)

   _____

7. *AD* = 1 and *DC* = 3. Find the perimeter of $\triangle ABC$. _____

8. Using the ratios you found in Problem 6 and the answer to Problem 7, find the perimeters of $\triangle ADB$ and $\triangle BDC$. perimeter of

   $\triangle ADB$: _____ perimeter of $\triangle BDC$: _____

LESSON
11-4

AA Similarity of Triangles

Practice and Problem Solving: A/B

For Problems 1 and 2, explain why the triangles are similar and write a similarity statement.

1.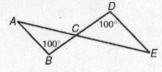

2.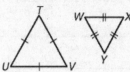

_____   _____

_____   _____

_____   _____

_____   _____

For Problems 3 and 4, verify that the triangles are similar. Explain why.

3. △JLK and △JMN

4. △PQR and △UTS

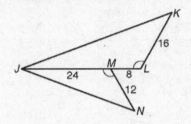
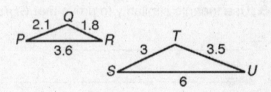

_____   _____

_____   _____

For Problem 5, explain why the triangles are similar and find the stated length.

5. DE

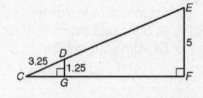

_____

_____

_____

LESSON 11-4

AA Similarity of Triangles

Practice and Problem Solving: C

Use principles of triangle similarity to solve Problems 1–4.

1. Find *ST*. Explain your reasoning.

_____

_____

_____

_____

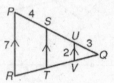

2. Triangle *ABC* is a right triangle. $\overline{BD}$ is perpendicular to $\overline{AC}$. Show that $\triangle ABC \sim \triangle ADB \sim \triangle BDC$.

_____

_____

_____

_____

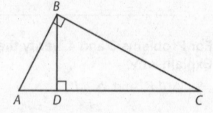

3. Use triangle similarity to prove that *GHIJK* ~ *PQRST*.

_____

_____

_____

_____

_____

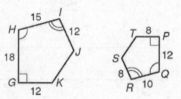

4. To measure the distance *EF* across the lake, a surveyor at *S* locates points *E, F, G,* and *H* as shown. Find *EF*. Explain your answer.

_____

_____

_____

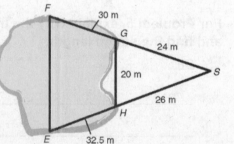

LESSON
12-1

Triangle Proportionality Theorem

Practice and Problem Solving: A/B

For Problems 1–4, find the value of *x*.

1.

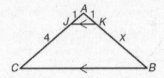

2.

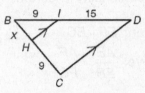

_____

_____

3.

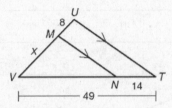

4.

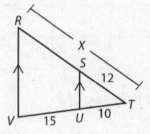

_____

_____

For Problems 5 and 6, determine whether the given segments are parallel.

5. $\overline{PQ}$ and $\overline{NM}$

_____

_____

_____

_____

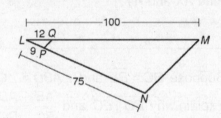

6. $\overline{WX}$ and $\overline{DE}$

_____

_____

_____

_____

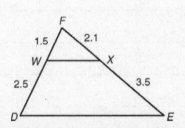

LESSON 12-1 **Triangle Proportionality Theorem**

Practice and Problem Solving: C

1. Write a paragraph proof of the Triangle Proportionality Theorem.

   Given: $\overline{EF} \parallel \overline{BC}$

   Prove: $\dfrac{AE}{EB} = \dfrac{AF}{FC}$

   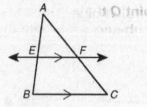

   _____

   _____

   _____

   _____

2. Find the value of *x*.

   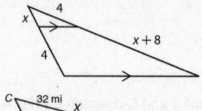

   _____

3. The perimeter of $\triangle ABC$ is 128 miles.

   Find *AX* and *AY*.

   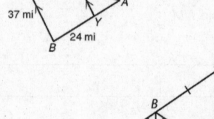

   _____

4. Suppose $\overline{BC} \cong \overline{BE}$ and $\angle ABD \cong \angle CBD$.

   Explain why $\overline{BD} \parallel \overline{EC}$ and $\dfrac{AB}{BC} = \dfrac{AD}{DC}$.

   _____

   _____

   _____

   _____

   _____

   _____

LESSON 12-2

Subdividing a Segment in a Given Ratio

Practice and Problem Solving: A/B

Find the coordinates of point *Q* that subdivides the segment with the given endpoints into two sub-segments with the given ratio. In each case, graph both the segment and the point *Q*.

1. endpoints: $A(-4, -2)$, $B(1, 8)$
   ratio: 4 to 1

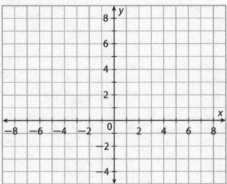

   Q (_____, _____)

2. endpoints: $S(-6, 6)$, $T(6, -2)$
   ratio: 1 to 4

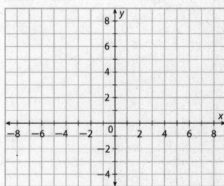

   Q (_____, _____)

3. endpoints: $G(-3, -4)$, $Z(0, 8)$
   ratio: 2 to 1

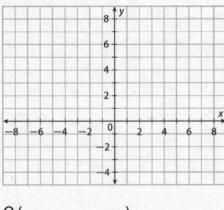

   Q (_____, _____)

4. endpoints: $J(-7, 2)$, $K(8, -3)$
   ratio: 2 to 3

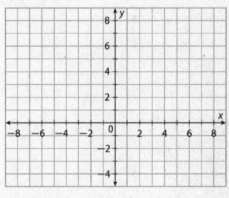

   Q (_____, _____)

Construct the point *P* that divides the segment into two sub-segments with the given ratio.

5. Ratio 2 to 1

6. Ratio 3 to 2

K ●————————● L

M ●————————● N

LESSON 12-2 Subdividing a Segment in a Given Ratio

Practice and Problem Solving: C

Find the coordinates of point Q that subdivides the segment with the given endpoints into two sub-segments with the given ratio. Round answers to the nearest tenth. Graph both the segment and the point Q.

1. endpoints: *A*(–6, 7), *B*(4, –4)
   ratio: 5 to 2

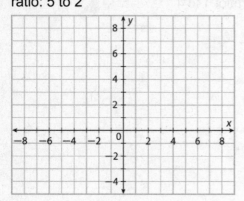

   Q (_____, _____)

2. endpoints: *Y*(–6, 2), *Z*(8, 8)
   ratio: 3 to 2

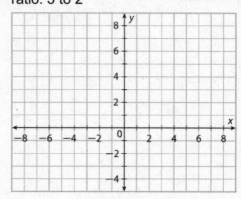

   Q (_____, _____)

3. endpoints: *D*(–3, 6), *E*(7, –3)
   ratio: 5 to 3

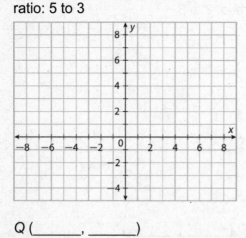

   Q (_____, _____)

4. endpoints: *R*(–7, 2), *S*(8, 3)
   ratio: 2 to 7

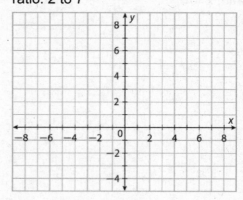

   Q (_____, _____)

Construct the point Q that divides the segment into two sub-segments with the given ratio.

5. Ratio 3 to 4

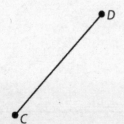

6. Ratio 5 to 1

LESSON 12-3

Using Proportional Relationships

Practice and Problem Solving: A/B

Refer to the figure for Problems 1–3. The figure shows triangles *ABC* and *DEF* formed by a person and a tree with their shadows. The figure is not drawn to scale.

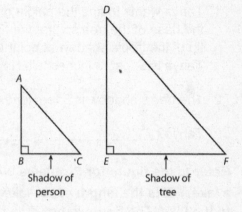

1. Jim, shown by $\overline{AB}$, is 5 feet, 8 inches tall. He casts a shadow that is 6 feet, 4 inches long. A tree, shown by $\overline{DE}$, casts a shadow that is 19 feet long. How tall is the tree? _____

2. Alicia is 5 feet, 4 inches tall. She casts a shadow that is 6 feet long. The tree casts a shadow that is 18 feet long. How tall is the tree?

    _____

3. Explain why triangles *ABC* and *DEF* are similar.

    _____

    _____

Refer to the figure for Problems 4–6. In the figure, $\overline{PQ}$ represents the width of a lake. $\overline{PQ}$ and $\overline{ST}$ are parallel. The figure is not drawn to scale.

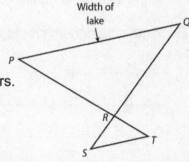

4. Suppose *PR* = 45 meters, *RT* = 16 meters, and *ST* = 24 meters. What is the width of the lake? _____

5. Suppose *QR* = 52 yards, *RS* = 15 yards, and *ST* = 20 yards. How wide is the lake? _____

Refer to the figure for Problems 6 and 7. A mirror is placed on the ground, shown by point *N*, so that a person looking at it can see the top of a nearby statue, shown by point *P*. The figure is not drawn to scale.

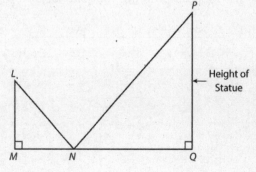

6. The mirror is placed 30 feet away from the statue, and Jean stands 5 feet from the mirror. If her eyes are 5 feet, 6 inches above the ground, shown by $\overline{LM}$, how tall is the statue?_____

7. The mirror is placed 5 meters away from the statue and Paul stands 1 meter from the mirror. If his eyes are 1.5 meters above the ground, how tall is the statue?_____

LESSON 12-3
Using Proportional Relationships
Practice and Problem Solving: C

Refer to the figure for Problems 1 and 2. The figure is not drawn to scale. $\overline{AB}$ **represents a tree and** $\overline{DE}$ **represents Tanya.**

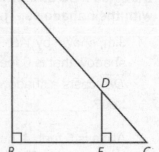

1. Tanya wants to find the height of the tree. She walks away from the base of the tree so that the tip of her shadow coincides with the tip of the tree's shadow at point *C*. *BE* is two and a half times *EC*. Tanya is 5 feet, 3 inches tall. How tall is the tree?_____

2. The tree's shadow is 8 feet long. How far from the tree is Tanya? _____

Refer to the figure for Problems 3–5. The oval represents a lake. *PQ* **is the length of the lake.** $\overline{UV}$ **is a road parallel to the lake. The figure is not drawn to scale.**

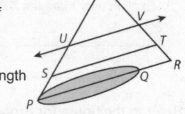

3. If *QR* = 30 m, *UV* = 40 m and 5*PU* = 4*UW*, what is the length of the lake?_____

4. In order to build a parallel road $\overline{ST}$ with a length equal to the length of the lake, what fraction of *PW* is *PS*?_____

5. Write a paragraph proof to show that △*WUV* is similar to △*WPR*.

_____

_____

_____

_____

6. The figure shows an overhead view of a square 10-foot-by-10-foot room. Maureen stands at point *M* and Nora stands at point *N*. They want to place mirrors at points *P* and *Q* so they can see each other in the reflections. Determine the values of *x* and *y*.

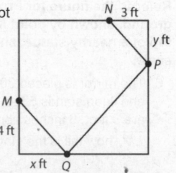

_____

Similarity in Right Triangles

Practice and Problem Solving: A/B

Write a similarity statement comparing the three triangles in each diagram.

1.

2.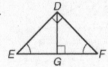

3.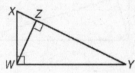

_____   _____   _____

_____

Find the geometric mean of each pair of numbers. If necessary, give the answer in simplest radical form.

4. $\dfrac{1}{4}$ and 4 _____

5. 3 and 75 _____

6. 4 and 18 _____

7. $\dfrac{1}{2}$ and 9 _____

8. 10 and 14 _____

9. 4 and 12.25 _____

Find x, y, and z.

10.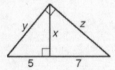

11.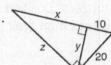

12.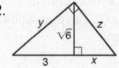

_____   _____   _____

13.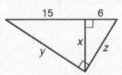

14.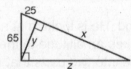

15.

_____   _____   _____

16. The Coast Guard has sent a rescue helicopter to retrieve passengers off a disabled ship. The ship has called in its position as 1.7 miles from shore. When the helicopter passes over a buoy that is known to be 1.3 miles from shore, the angle formed by the shore, the helicopter, and the disabled ship is 90°. Determine what the altimeter would read to the nearest foot when the helicopter is directly above the buoy. Note that 1 mile is 5280 feet.

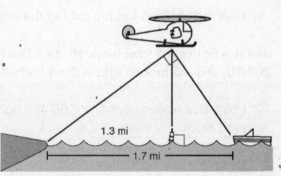

_____

Name _____ Date _____ Class _____

Similarity in Right Triangles

Practice and Problem Solving: C

Find x and y.

1.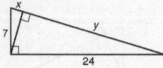

   _____

2.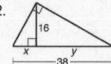

   _____

3.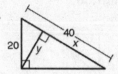

   _____

4. The *arithmetic mean* is also known as the average. Name the conditions under which two nonzero, positive numbers, *a* and *b*, have equal geometric and arithmetic means.

   _____

5. Sketch a right triangle in which the segments of the hypotenuse formed by the altitude to the hypotenuse have the same geometric and arithmetic means.

6. Give all three angle measures of the triangle you drew in Problem 5. _____

7. Name the conditions under which two nonzero, positive numbers, *a* and *b*, have an arithmetic mean that is less than their geometric mean.

   _____

   _____

Greg is interested in buying a plot of land. He is looking at a plot in the shape of a right triangle. A dirt road makes an altitude to the longest side of the plot and cuts the longest side into two parts that measure 65 feet and 83 feet.

8. Find the area of the land to the nearest square foot.   _____

9. Find the perimeter of the land to the nearest foot.   _____

Use the figure for Problems 10–12. The figure shows △ABC. AB = 3 inches and AC = 4 inches.

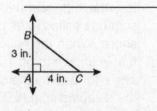

10. Point *D* is placed so that ∠CBD is a right angle and *D* is on $\overline{AC}$. Find *BD*.

    _____

11. Point *E* is placed so that ∠BCE is a right angle and *E* is on $\overline{AB}$. Find *CE*.

    _____

12. Find *DE*.

    _____

Name _____ Date _____ Class_____

Tangent Ratio

Practice and Problem Solving: A/B

Identify the relationships in the figure to the right.

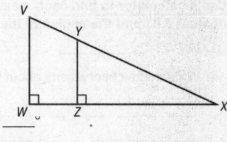

1. $\tan X = \dfrac{\square}{WX} = \dfrac{\square}{\square}$

2. $\tan V = \dfrac{\square}{\square}$

3. $\tan^{-1} \dfrac{VW}{WX} = m\angle$_____

4. $\tan^{-1} \dfrac{WX}{VW} = m\angle$_____

5. $\tan X \times \tan V =$ _____

6. $\tan^{-1} \dfrac{VW}{WX} + \tan^{-1} \dfrac{WX}{VW} =$ _____

Use a calculator to find each tangent or inverse tangent. Round tangents to the nearest 0.01 and angles to the nearest 0.1 degree. Check the inverse tangents by finding the tangent of each angle.

7. $\tan 23° \approx$ _____

8. $\tan 43° \approx$ _____

9. $\tan 47° \approx$ _____

10. $\tan^{-1} 0.14 \approx$ _____ °

11. $\tan^{-1} 1 =$ _____ °

12. $\tan^{-1} 6.1 \approx$ _____ °

$\tan$ _____ ° ≈ 0.14

$\tan$ _____ ° $= 1$

$\tan$ _____ ° ≈ 6.1

Solve Problems 13–16 using tangent ratios and a calculator. Refer to the figure to the right of each problem.

13. To the nearest hundredth, what is $\tan M$ in $\triangle LMN$? _____

14. Write a ratio that gives $\tan S$. _____ Find the value of $\tan S$ to

   the nearest hundredth. _____ Use the inverse tangent function

   on your calculator to find the angle with that tangent. _____

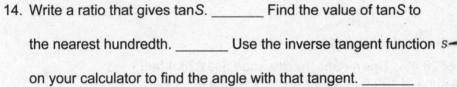

15. Write and solve a tangent equation to find the distance from

   C to E to the nearest 0.1 meter. _____ meters

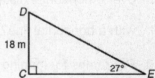

16. The glide slope is the path a plane uses while it is landing
   on a runway. The glide slope usually makes a 3° angle with
   the ground. A plane is on the glide slope and is 1 mile (5280 feet)
   from touchdown. Find EF, the plane's altitude, to the
   nearest foot. Show your work.

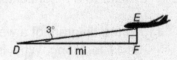

_____

_____

Name _____ Date _____ Class_____

Tangent Ratio
Practice and Problem Solving: C

Use a calculator to find each measure. Round the tangent to the nearest 0.01 and the angles to the nearest 0.1 degree.

1. $\tan 13° \approx$ _____

2. $\tan^{-1} 1.15 \approx$ _____

3. $\tan^{-1} 57.3 \approx$ _____

4. Write some observations about the size of an angle, $a°$, and its tangent.

_____

A Pythagorean triple is a set of positive integers that satisfies the Pythagorean Theorem. Problems 5–8 show Pythagorean triples. Use tangent ratios to find the measures of the two acute angles, to the nearest degree, in triangles with sides of these lengths. For Problem 5, show your work, including two ways to find the second angle.

5. 3-4-5

$m\angle A =$ _____

$m\angle A =$ _____

6. 5-12-13

$m\angle A =$ _____

$m\angle B =$ _____

7. 8-15-17

$m\angle A =$ _____

$m\angle B =$ _____

8. 7-24-25

$m\angle A =$ _____

$m\angle B =$ _____

Use tangent ratios to solve Problems 9–12.

9. A road has a grade of 28.4%. This means that the road rises 28.4 feet over a horizontal distance of 100 feet. What angle does the hill make with a horizontal line? Round to the nearest degree. _____

10. Pet ramps for loading dogs into vehicles usually have slopes between $\frac{2}{5}$ and $\frac{1}{2}$. What is the range of angle measures that these pet ramps make with a horizontal line? Round to the nearest degree. _____

11. In the diagram of a waterslide, the ladder, represented by $\overline{AB}$, is 17 feet long. What is the length of the slide, to the nearest 0.1 foot? _____

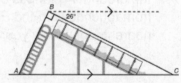

12. Right triangle ABC is graphed on the coordinate plane and has vertices at A(−1, 3), B(0, 5), and C(4, 3). Show how you could use a tangent ratio to find the measure of $\angle C$ to the nearest degree.

_____

_____

LESSON 13-2

Sine and Cosine Ratios

Practice and Problem Solving: A/B

After verifying that the triangle to the right is a right triangle, use a calculator to find the given measures. Give ratios to the nearest hundredth and angles to the nearest degree.

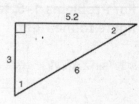

1. Use the Pythagorean Theorem to confirm that the triangle is a right triangle. Show your work.

   _____

2. $\sin\angle 1 = \dfrac{\Box}{\Box} \approx$ _____

3. $\sin\angle 2 = \dfrac{\Box}{\Box} =$ _____

4. $\cos\angle 1 = \dfrac{\Box}{\Box} =$ _____

5. $\cos\angle 2 = \dfrac{\Box}{\Box} \approx$ _____

6. Show how to find m$\angle 1$ using the inverse sine of $\angle 1$.

   _____

7. Show how to find m$\angle 2$ using the inverse sine of $\angle 2$.

   _____

Use a calculator and trigonometric ratios to find each length. Round to the nearest hundredth.

8.

   $BD =$ _____

9.

   $QP =$ _____

10.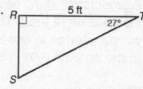

    $ST =$ _____

Use sine and cosine ratios to solve Problems 11–13.

11. Find the perimeter of the triangle. Round to the nearest

    0.1 centimeter. _____

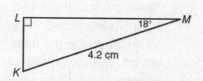

12. To the nearest 0.1 inch, what is the length of the hypotenuse

    of the springboard shown to the right? _____

13. What is the height of the springboard (the dotted

    line)? _____

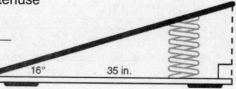

LESSON
13-2

Sine and Cosine Ratios

Practice and Problem Solving: C

For Problems 1–5, tell the trigonometric relationships in the figure to the right.

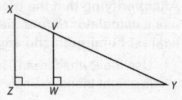

1. $\sin\angle YVW = \dfrac{\square}{\square} = \dfrac{\square}{\square}$

2. $\sin\angle Y = \dfrac{\square}{\square} = \dfrac{\square}{\square}$

3. Simplify: $\sin Y - \cos Y = $ _____

4. Simplify: $\dfrac{\sin Y}{\cos Y} = $ _____

5. Simplify as much as possible (to a single number): $(\cos Y)^2 + (\sin Y)^2$. Show your work and explain your reasoning.

_____

_____

Use trigonometric ratios to solve Problems 6–9. Show your work in the space to the right of each problem.

6. The steepness, or grade, of a road or a ramp can be given as a percent. The grade of a treadmill ramp is 7%, which means that it would rise 7 inches over a horizontal distance of 100 inches. If the length of the ramp itself is 53 inches, to the nearest 0.1 inch, how many inches does it rise vertically? Show your work. _____

7. A wheelchair ramp has a slope of 1:12 (1 foot of rise over a horizontal distance of 12 feet). To the nearest 0.1 foot, how many feet of ramp will be needed to rise 3 feet? (Round the angle of incline to the nearest 0.01°.) Show your work. _____

8. The hypotenuse of a right triangle measures 9 inches, and one of the acute angles measures 36°. To the nearest square inch, what is the area of the triangle? Show your work. _____

9. Given the lengths of two sides of any triangle and the measure of the included angle, the area of the triangle can be found. In the figure, suppose the lengths b and c and the measure of $\angle A$ are known. Develop a formula for finding the area. Explain your answer. (*Hint:* Draw an altitude.)

_____

_____

_____

LESSON
13-3

Special Right Triangles
Practice and Problem Solving: A/B

**Use the figure to the right for Problems 1–4. Write each
trigonometric ratio as a simplified fraction and as a decimal
rounded to the nearest hundredth.**

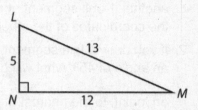

1. sin*L*

_____

2. cos*L*

_____

3. tan*M*

_____

4. sin*M*

_____

Write each trigonometric ratio as a simplified fraction.

5. sin 30° = _____

6. cos 30° = _____

7. tan 45° = _____

8. tan 30° = _____

9. cos 45° = _____

10. tan 60° = _____

11. Fill in the side lengths for these special right triangles with a
    hypotenuse of 1. Use decimals to the nearest 0.01, and be sure that
    your answers make sense, for example that the hypotenuse is longer
    than the legs.

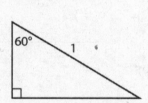

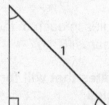

Use special right triangle relationships to solve Problems 12–14.

12. If cos *A* = 0.28, which angle in the triangles to the

    right is ∠*A*? _____

    If sin *B* = 0.22, which angle is ∠*B*? _____

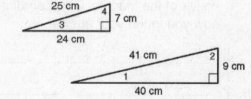

13. What is *EF*, the measure of the longest side of the sail

    on the model? Round to the nearest inch. _____ in.

    What is the measure of the shortest side? _____ in.

14. If the small sail is similar to the larger one and is 11

    inches high, about how wide is it? _____ in.

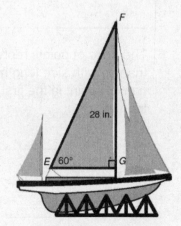

Special Right Triangles

Practice and Problem Solving: C

Use special right triangle relationships to solve Problems 1–4.

1. On the coordinate plane, draw a line segment from the origin at a 30° angle to the *x*-axis. Label it 1 unit. Draw another 1-unit segment at a 150° angle to the *x*-axis. Label the coordinates of the other endpoint of each segment.

2. If you draw a line segment 5 units long from the origin at an angle of 45°, what will be the coordinates of the other

   endpoint, to the nearest 0.1 unit? (_____, _____)

3. Find the missing number in each set of Pythagorean triples. For each set, write an equation to show that the three integers form the three sides of a right triangle.

   12, 13, and _____

   12, 16, and _____

   12, 37, and _____

4. Find the measures of the two acute angles in each of the triangles in Problem 3. Give your answers to the nearest 0.1°.   _____

For Problems 5 and 6, name the coordinates that will form triangles whose side lengths are Pythagorean triples.

5. The points (0, 0) and (5, 0) are the endpoints of the hypotenuse of a right triangle. Name a point in the first quadrant that forms the third vertex of the triangle. Give coordinates to the nearest 0.01. Explain how you found your answer.

   _____

   _____

   _____

6. The pairs of points represent the endpoints of the hypotenuse of a right triangle with side lengths that form a Pythagorean triple. For each pair, name a point in the first quadrant that forms the third vertex of the triangle.

   (0, 0), (13, 0), (_____, _____)

   (0, 0), (17, 0), (_____, _____)

   (0, 0), (25, 0), (_____, _____)

LESSON 13-4

Problem Solving with Trignometry

Practice and Problem Solving: A/B

Use a calculator and inverse trigonometric ratios to find the unknown side lengths and angle measures. Round lengths to the nearest hundredth and angle measures to the nearest degree.

1.

AC = _____

m∠B = _____

m∠C = _____

2.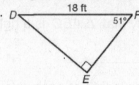

DE = _____

EF = _____

m∠D = _____

3.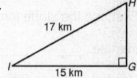

GH = _____

m∠H = _____

m∠I = _____

△*XYZ* has vertices *X*(6, 6), *Y*(6, 3), and *Z*(1, 3). Complete Problems 4–6 to find the side lengths to the nearest hundredth and the angle measures to the nearest degree.

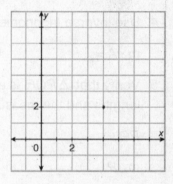

4. Plot the points and draw △*XYZ*.

5. Find *XY* and *YZ* from the graph. Use the Pythagorean Theorem to find *XZ*.

   XY = _____   YZ = _____   XZ = _____

6. Find the angle measures.

   m∠X _____   m∠Z _____

For each triangle, find all three side lengths to the nearest hundredth and all three angle measures to the nearest degree.

7. *B*(–2, –4), *C*(3, 3), *D*(–2, 3) _____

8. *L*(–1, –6), *M*(1, –6), *N*(–1, 1) _____

9. *X*(–4, 5), *Y*(–3, 5), *Z*(–3, 4) _____

Follow the steps to find the area of the triangle using trigonometry.

10. Draw a line from vertex *U* perpendicular to the base $\overline{TV}$ at a point *W*. Label its length *h*. Write the sine of ∠*T* as a ratio using variables in the figure. Solve for *h*. Then write the area of the triangle using your value for *h*.

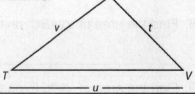

   sin*T* = ▭   *h* = _____   *Area* = _____

   | Area of a triangle = $\frac{1}{2}$ base × height |

11. What is the area of the triangle if ∠*T* = 37°, *u* = 14, and *v* = 10? _____

Problem Solving with Trignometry

Practice and Problem Solving: C

For Problems 1–6, use trigonometry and the Pythagorean theorem to solve the right triangles on the coordinate plane. Show your work.

1. First use the slope formula to verify that △*ABC* is a right

   triangle. _____

2. Use the distance formula to find the length of each side.

   AB = _____   *BC* = _____   *AC* = _____

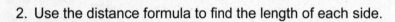

3. Use the Pythagorean theorem to double check the side

   lengths. _____

4. Use inverse trigonometric ratios to find the acute angles.

   m∠*A* = _____   m∠*C* = _____

5. Verify that △*PQR* is a right triangle. Find the three side
   lengths and the measures of the acute angles.

   PQ = _____   *QR* = _____   *RP* = _____

   m∠*P* = _____   m∠*Q* = _____

6. Find the side lengths and angle measures for △*XYZ*,
   X(1, 0), *Y*(2, 1), *Z*(5, –2).

   XY = _____   *YZ* = _____   *XZ* = _____

   m∠*X* = _____   m∠*Y* = _____   m∠*Z* = _____

For Problems 7–10, use trigonometric functions to find the area of the triangles, to the nearest square unit.

7. If you know the lengths of two sides of any triangle, *a* and *b*, and
   the measure of the included angle, m∠*C*, how can you find the

   area of the triangle? _____

8. Find the area of △*ABC* on the coordinate plane above.

   _____

9. Find the area of △*PQR* on the coordinate plane above.

   _____

10. Find the area of △*XYZ* in Problem 6 above. _____

Name _____ Date _____ Class_____

LESSON
14-1

Law of Sines

Practice and Problem Solving: A/B

Find the measures indicated. Round to the nearest tenth.

1.
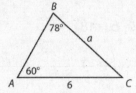

a = _____   m∠C = _____

2.
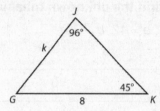

k = _____   m∠G = _____

3.
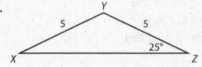

m∠X = _____   m∠Y = _____

4.
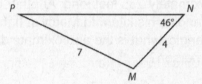

m∠P = _____   m∠M = _____

5.
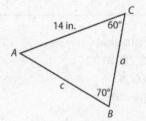

c = ____ m∠A = ____ a = ____

6.
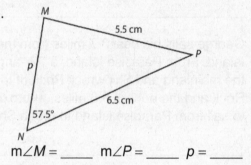

m∠M = ____ m∠P = ____ p = ____

Determine how many triangles are possible and find the unknown measures. Round to the nearest tenth.

7. m∠B = 145°, a = 8, b = 22

8. m∠C = 75°, a = 8, c = 5

_____

_____

_____

_____

Name _____ Date _____ Class_____

Law of Sines

Practice and Problem Solving: C

Determine how many triangles are possible with the given measures and find the unknown measures.

1. $m\angle A = 107°$, $a = 42$, $b = 25$ 2. $m\angle B = 65°$, $c = 19$, $b = 18$

_____   _____

_____   _____

_____   _____

3. Marcy flies her kite at a 45° angle from the ground. The kite string is approximately 235 feet long. Another person on the other side of the park tangles his kite with Marcy's. If the other person is flying his kite at a 72°angle, what is the approximate distance between Marcy and the other person?

_____

_____

_____

4. George sails his boat 3.7 miles from the dock at the mainland to Paradise Island. From Paradise Island, a 72° angle is formed between the dock at the mainland and Shipwreck Rock. If the distance between Shipwreck Rock and the dock is 5.6 miles, approximately how far does George need to sail from Paradise Island to reach Shipwreck Rock?

_____

_____

_____

LESSON 14-2

Law of Cosines

Practice and Problem Solving: A/B

Find the measures indicated. Round to the nearest tenth.

1.

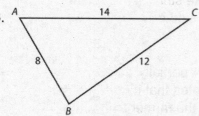

$S =$ _____

2.

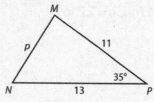

$p =$ _____

3.

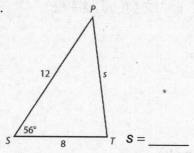

$m\angle A =$ ____ $m\angle B =$ ____ $m\angle C =$ ____

4.

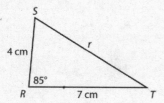

$m\angle X =$ ____ $m\angle Y =$ ____ $m\angle Z =$ ____

5.

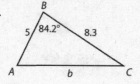

$r =$ ____ $m\angle S =$ ____ $m\angle T =$ ____

6.

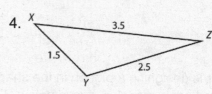

$m\angle W =$ ____ $m\angle U =$ ____ $m\angle V =$ ____

Determine whether there is enough information to use the Law of Cosines to solve for the triangle. Explain how you know.

7.

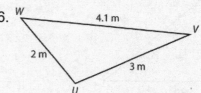

8.

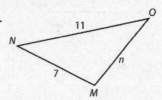

9.

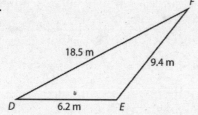

10.

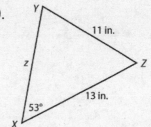

LESSON 14-2

Law of Cosines

Practice and Problem Solving: C

Solve each triangle. Round to the nearest tenth.

1. $a = 14$ in, $b = 17$ in, $c = 22$ in

2. $x = 9.2$ ft, $y = 12.7$ ft, $m\angle Z = 65°$

3. A farmer is designing a pigpen in the shape of a triangle. A partially
   completed scale model is shown below. The farmer estimates that it
   will cost $24 per yard for fencing. How much would it cost the farmer to
   build the entire fence?

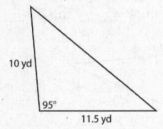

10 yd

95°

11.5 yd

4. Solve for *x* using the figure below.

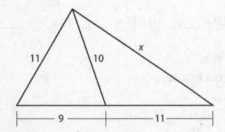

11   10   *x*

9   11

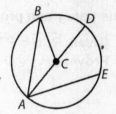

LESSON 15-1 Central Angles and Inscribed Angles

Practice and Problem Solving: A/B

Refer to the figure for Problems 1–3. *C* is the center of the circle.

1. Name the chord(s). _____

2. Name the central angle(s). _____

3. Name the inscribed angle(s). _____

For each figure, determine the indicated measures.

4. 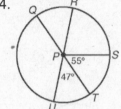 m$\widehat{QS}$ = _____

   m$\widehat{RQT}$ = _____

5. 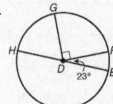 m$\widehat{HG}$ = _____

   m$\widehat{FEH}$ = _____

6. 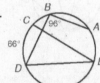 m∠CED = _____

   m$\widehat{DEA}$ = _____

7.   m∠FGI = _____

   m$\widehat{GH}$ = _____

Find the unknown value.

8. 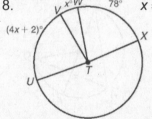 x = _____

9. 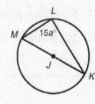 a = _____

The figure shows a passenger airplane's flight path on a circular radar screen in an air traffic control tower.

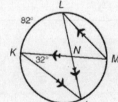

10. What is m$\widehat{MJ}$? _____

11. What is m∠LJK? _____

12. What is m∠LNK? _____

LESSON
15-1

Central Angles and Inscribed Angles
Practice and Problem Solving: C

Write paragraph proofs for Problems 1 and 2.

1. **Given:** $\overset{\frown}{RSU} \cong \overset{\frown}{RTU}$
   Prove: $\odot P \cong \odot Q$

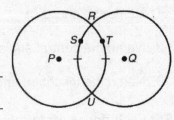

   _____

   _____

   _____

   _____

2. **Given:** $\overline{AC} \cong \overline{AD}$
   Prove: $\angle ABC \cong \angle AED$

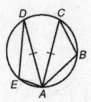

   _____

   _____

   _____

   _____

3. In $\odot C$, $\triangle ABE \sim \triangle CDE$. Find the measures for $\angle BAE$, $\angle EBA$, and $\angle BEA$. Explain how you got your answers.

   _____

   _____

   _____

LESSON
15-2

Angles in Inscribed Quadrilaterals

Practice and Problem Solving: A/B

Each quadrilateral described is inscribed in a circle. Determine the angle measures.

1. Quadrilateral *ABCD* has m∠*A* = 53° and m∠*B* = 82°.

   m∠*C* = _____   m∠*D* = _____

2. Quadrilateral *RSTU* has m∠*S* = 104° and m∠*T* = 55°.

   m∠*R* = _____ .   m∠*U* = _____

3. Quadrilateral *JKLM* has m∠*J* = 90° and ∠*K* ≅ ∠*M*.

   m∠*K* = _____   m∠*L* = _____   m∠*M* = _____

Determine whether each quadrilateral can be inscribed in a circle. If it cannot be determined, say so.

4. 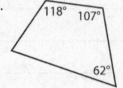 _____

5. 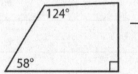 _____

6. 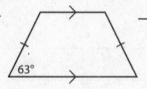 _____

7.   _____

For each inscribed quadrilateral, determine the angle measures.

8.

   m∠*X* = _____

   m∠*Y* = _____

   m∠*Z* = _____

   m∠*W* = _____

9.

   m∠*C* = _____

   m∠*D* = _____

   m∠*E* = _____

   m∠*F* = _____

10.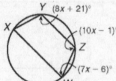

   m∠*T* = _____

   m∠*U* = _____

   m∠*V* = _____

   m∠*W* = _____

11.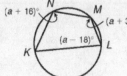

   m∠*K* = _____

   m∠*L* = _____

   m∠*M* = _____

   m∠*N* = _____

LESSON
15-2

Angles in Inscribed Quadrilaterals

Practice and Problem Solving: C

For each inscribed quadrilateral, find the measure of its angles.

1.

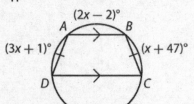

$m\angle A =$ _____

$m\angle B =$ _____

$m\angle C =$ _____

$m\angle D =$ _____

2.

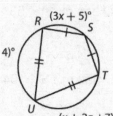

$m\angle R =$ _____

$m\angle S =$ _____

$m\angle T =$ _____

$m\angle U =$ _____

For each quadrilateral described, tell whether it can be inscribed in a circle. If so, describe a method for doing so using a compass and straightedge. Then draw an example.

3. a parallelogram that is not a rectangle or a square

_____

_____

_____

_____

4. a kite

_____

_____

_____

_____

5. a trapezoid

_____

_____

_____

_____

LESSON 15-3

Tangents and Circumscribed Angles
Practice and Problem Solving: A/B

Refer to the figure for Problems 1–4. $\overline{AB}$ **is tangent to** $\odot C$
at point *B* **and** $\overline{AD}$ **is tangent to** $\odot C$ **at point** *B*. **Determine**
the angle measures.

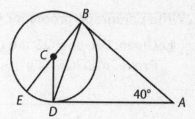

1. m∠*ABC* = _____   2. m∠*DCB* = _____

3. m∠*BDA* = _____   4. m∠*CDB* = _____

Refer to the figure for Problems 5–8. $\overline{AB}$ **is tangent to**
$\odot C$ **at point** *B* **and** $\overline{AD}$ **is tangent to** $\odot C$ **at point** *B*.
Determine the angle measures.

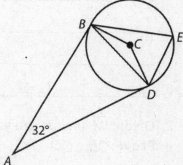

5. m∠*BCD* = _____   6. m∠*CDA* = _____

7. m∠*BED* = _____   8. m∠*DBA* = _____

In Problems 9 and 10, $\overline{QM}$ **is tangent to** $\odot P$ **at point** *M* **and** $\overline{QN}$ **is**
tangent to $\odot P$ **at point** *P*. **Solve for the variable and determine the**
angle measures.

9.

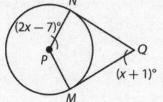

x = _____   m∠*NQM* = _____

m∠*PNQ* = _____   m∠*NPM* = _____

10.

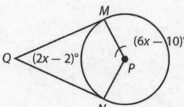

x = _____   m∠*MQN* = _____

m∠*QMP* = _____   m∠*NPM* = _____

In Problems 11 and 12, $\overline{EF}$ **is tangent to** $\odot H$ **at point** *F* **and** $\overline{EG}$ **is**
tangent to $\odot H$ **at point** *G*. **Determine the length of** $\overline{EF}$.

11.

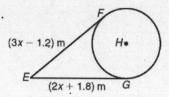

EF = _____   12.

EF = _____

LESSON
15-3

Tangents and Circumscribed Angles

Practice and Problem Solving: C

Write paragraph proofs for Problems 1 and 2.

1. **Given:** $\overline{QR}$ and $\overline{QS}$ are tangent to $\odot P$; $\angle PQR \cong \angle TUS$.
   Prove: $m\angle RQS = 60°$

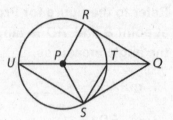

_____

_____

_____

_____

_____

2. **Given:** $\overline{IM}$ and $\overline{JL}$ are tangent to $\odot G$ and $\odot H$.
   Prove: $\odot P \cong \odot Q$

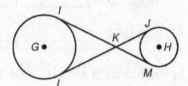

_____

_____

_____

_____

_____

In Problems 3 and 4, assume that the segments appearing to be tangent are tangent. Determine the length.

3.

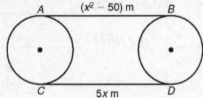

4.

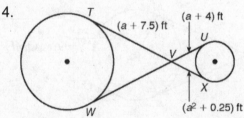

$CD =$ _____ $UW =$ _____

LESSON
15-4

Segment Relationships in Circles

Practice and Problem Solving: A/B

For each figure, determine the value of the variable and the indicated lengths by applying the Chord-Chord Product Theorem.

1.

$x =$ _____

$AD =$ _____

$BE =$ _____

2.

$y =$ _____

$FH =$ _____

$GI =$ _____

3.

$z =$ _____

$PS =$ _____

$RT =$ _____

4.

$m =$ _____

$UW =$ _____

$VX =$ _____

For each figure, determine the value of the variable and the indicated lengths by applying the Secant-Secant Product Theorem.

5.

$x =$ _____

$BD =$ _____

$FD =$ _____

6.

$y =$ _____

$GJ =$ _____

$GK =$ _____

7.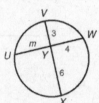

$z =$ _____

$SQ =$ _____

$SU =$ _____

8.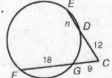

$n =$ _____

$CE =$ _____

$CF =$ _____

For each figure, determine the value of the variable and the indicated length by applying the Secant-Tangent Product Theorem.

9.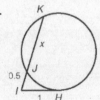

$x =$ _____

$1K =$ _____

10.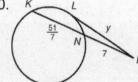

$y =$ _____

$KM =$ _____

LESSON
15-4
Segment Relationships in Circles
Practice and Problem Solving: C

For each figure, determine the value of x. Write your answers in simplest radical form if necessary.

1.
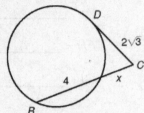
x = _____

2.
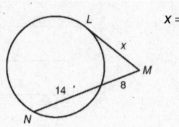
x = _____

3.
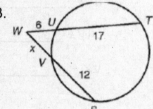
x = _____

4.
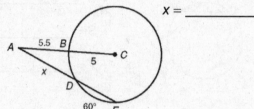
x = _____

5.
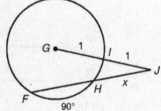
x = _____

6.
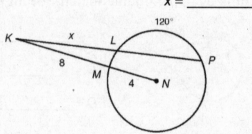
x = _____

For each figure, determine the indicated length.

7.
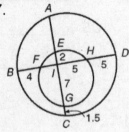
AC = _____

BD = _____

8.
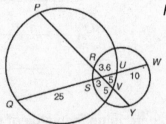
PY = _____

Name _____ Date _____ Class_____

Angle Relationships in Circles
Practice and Problem Solving: A/B

For each figure, determine the measure of the angle by applying the Intersecting Chords Angle Measure Theorem.

1.   m∠RPS = _____

2. 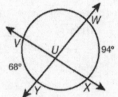   m∠YUV = _____

For each figure, determine the measures of the indicated angle and arc by applying the Tangent-Secant Interior Angle Measure Theorem.

3. 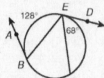   m∠ABE = _____

    mĈE = _____

4. 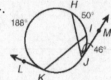   m∠LKI = _____

    mÎJ = _____

For each figure, determine the value of x by applying the Tangent-Secant Exterior Angle Measure Theorem.

5. 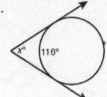   x = _____

6. 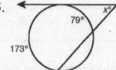   x = _____

7. 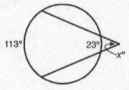   x = _____

8.   x = _____

For each figure, determine the measure of the intercepted minor arc.

9. 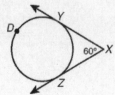   mŶZ = _____

10.   mD̂E = _____

Name _____ Date _____ Class_____

LESSON 15-5

Angle Relationships in Circles

Practice and Problem Solving: C

For each figure, determine the indicated angle and arc measures.

1.

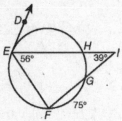

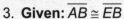

m∠DEI = _____

m$\widehat{EF}$ = _____

2.

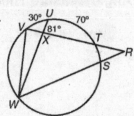

m∠WVR = _____

m$\widehat{TUW}$ = _____

Write paragraph proofs for Problems 3 and 4.

3. **Given:** $\overline{AB} \cong \overline{EB}$

   Prove: m$\widehat{DE}$ = 2m$\widehat{BC}$

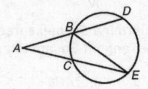

_____

_____

_____

_____

_____

_____

4. **Given:** $\overline{JK}$ and $\overline{JM}$ are tangents to the circle.

   Prove: m$\widehat{KM}$ < 180°

   (*Hint:* Use an indirect proof and consider two cases.)

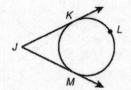

_____

_____

_____

_____

_____

_____

Name _____ Date _____ Class_____

Justifying Circumference and Area of a Circle
Practice and Problem Solving: A/B

For each figure, calculate the indicated circumference or area.
Give your answers in terms of π.

1.

   the circumference of ⊙V

   _____

2.

   the circumference of ⊙H

   _____

3.

   the area of ⊙M

   _____

4.

   the area of ⊙H

   _____

For Problems 5 and 6, determine the indicated measures.

5. What is the radius of a circle with a circumference of 2π centimeters? _____

6. What is the diameter of a circle with an area of 16π square meters? _____

Stella wants to cover a tabletop with nickels, dimes, or quarters.
She decides to find which coin would cost the least to use.

7. Stella measures the diameters of a nickel, a dime, and a quarter. They
   are 21.2 mm, 17.8 mm, and 24.5 mm, respectively. Find the areas of
   each coin. Round to the nearest tenth.

   _____

8. Divide each coin's value in cents by the coin's area. Round to nearest
   hundredth.

   _____

9. Which coin has the least value per unit of area? _____

LESSON 16-1 Justifying Circumference and Area of a Circle

Practice and Problem Solving: C

To estimate the circumference and area of a circle with a radius of 2 inches, cut out a square with side lengths of 4 inches. Place the circle in the square and cut diagonally at 45° angles at the corners as shown. The result is an octagon.

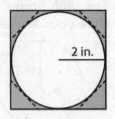

1. Find the perimeter of the octagon to estimate the circumference of the circle. Round to the nearest tenth.

_____

2. Find the area of the octagon to estimate the circumference of the circle. Round to the nearest tenth.

_____

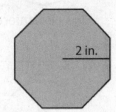

3. Use the formulas for circumference and area to find the actual circumference and area. Round to the nearest tenth. How do your answers compare?

_____

4. Observe that the octagon is regular and circumscribes the circle. Using θ and r, as shown in the figure, write a formula for the perimeter of the octagon. (*Hint*: Use trigonometric ratios.)

_____

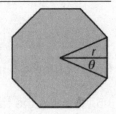

5. Next, write a formula for the area.   _____

6. Write general formulas for the perimeter and area of an *n*-gon that circumscribes a circle with the radius *r*. For *n*-gons, $\theta = \dfrac{360°}{2n} = \dfrac{180°}{n}$.

_____

_____

7. How do your formulas compare with formulas for the perimeter and the area of inscribed regular polygons?

_____

_____

LESSON 16-2 Arc Length and Radian Measure

Practice and Problem Solving: A/B

For each figure, calculate the length of the arc. Give your answer in terms of π and rounded to the nearest hundredth.

1.
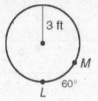

$\widehat{LM}$ _____

2.
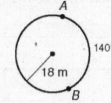

$\widehat{AB}$ _____

3.
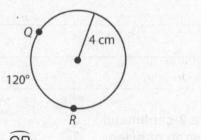

$\widehat{QR}$ _____

4.
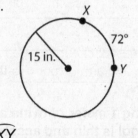

$\widehat{XY}$ _____

5. What is the length of an arc with a measure of 45°

   in circle with a diameter of 4 miles? _____

6. What is the length of an arc with a measure of

   120° in a circle with a diameter of 30 millimeters? _____

7. The minute hand on an analog clock is 6 inches long. How far does the tip of the minute hand travel as time goes from 6:35 to 6:45? Round to the nearest tenth.   _____

8. The minute hand on an analog clock is 8 inches long. How far does the tip of the minute hand travel as time goes from 1:27 to 1:43? Round to the nearest tenth.   _____

Change the given angle measure from degrees to radians.

9. 10° _____   10. 225° _____

11. 144° _____   12. 50° _____

LESSON 16-2

Arc Length and Radian Measure

Practice and Problem Solving: C

1. Find the measure of the central of an arc so that the length of the arc is equal to the radius of the circle. Round to the nearest tenth. Explain your answer. Then convert the angle into radians.

   _____

   _____

   _____

   _____

   _____

   _____

   _____

Angela is wrapping 1 meter of twine around a spool with a 2-centimeter diameter. The spool is thin and accommodates only one wrap of twine before the twine stacks on top of itself. The twine has a diameter of $\frac{1}{2}$ centimeter.

2. Find how many complete times Angela will wrap the twine around the spool.

   _____

3. Find the percentage of a complete circle that the last wrapping of the twine will make. Round to the nearest tenth.

   _____

4. $\overline{AB}$ and $\overline{AD}$ are tangents to $\odot C$. Find the perimeter of the figure. Show your work.

   _____

   _____

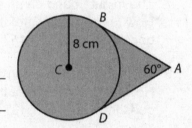

   _____

   _____

   _____

   _____

LESSON
16-3

Sector Area

Practice and Problem Solving: A/B

For each figure, calculate the area of the sector. Give your answers in terms of π and rounded to the nearest hundredth.

1.
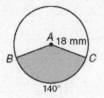

sector *BAC* _____

2.
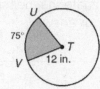

sector *UTV* _____

3.

sector *KJL* _____

4.
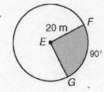

sector *FEG* _____

5. The speedometer needle in Ignacio's car is 2 inches long. The needle sweeps out a 130° sector during acceleration from 0 to 60 miles per hour. What is the area of the sector? Round to the nearest hundredth.

_____

For each figure, calculate the area of the shaded region rounded to the nearest hundredth.

6.

_____

7.

_____

8.

_____

9.
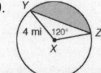

_____

LESSON
16-3

Sector Area

Practice and Problem Solving: C

1. Find the measure of a central angle in a circle so that the segment has half the area of the sector. First derive an equation, and then use trial and error to estimate the measure of the central angle to within 1 degree. Explain your answer.

_____

_____

_____

_____

_____

_____

2. The circumference of a circle is 18π meters. Find the central

   angle of a sector of the circle whose area is 40.5π m². _____

For each figure, calculate the area of the shaded region rounded to the nearest hundredth.

3.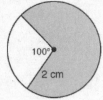

_____

4.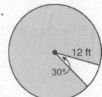

_____

5.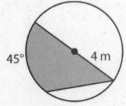

_____

6.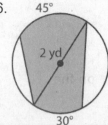

_____

LESSON 17-1

Equation of a Circle

Practice and Problem Solving: A/B

Write the equation of each circle.

1. Circle *X* centered at the origin with radius 10 _____

2. Circle *R* with center *R*(−1, 8) and radius 5 _____

3. Circle *P* with center *P*(−5, −5) and radius $2\sqrt{5}$ _____

4. Circle *O* centered at the origin that passes through (9, −2) _____

5. Circle *B* with center *B*(0, −2) that passes through (−6, 0) _____

Graph each equation.

6. $x^2 + y^2 = 25$

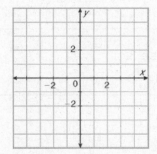

7. $(x + 2)^2 + (y − 1)^2 = 4$

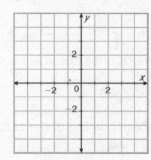

8. $x^2 + (y + 3)^2 = 1$

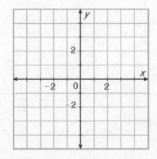

9. $(x − 1)^2 + (y − 1)^2 = 16$

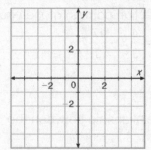

Crater Lake in Oregon is a roughly circular lake. The lake basin formed about 7000 years ago when the top of a volcano exploded in an immense explosion. Hillman Peak, Garfield Peak, and Cloudcap are three mountain peaks on the rim of the lake. The peaks are located in a coordinate plane at *H*(−4, 1), *G*(−2, −3), and *C*(5, −2).

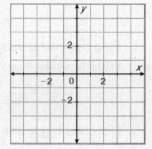

10. Find the coordinates of the center of the lake.

_____

11. Each unit of the coordinate plane represents $\frac{3}{5}$ mile.

Find the diameter of the lake. _____

LESSON 17-1
Equation of a Circle
Practice and Problem Solving: C

1. Points *A*, *B*, and *C* lie on the circumference of a circle. *AB* is twice the radius of the circle. Find m∠*ACB*.

   _____

2. Points *A*, *B*, and *C* lie on the circumference of a circle. The center of the circle lies in the exterior of △*ABC*. Classify △*ABC* by its angles.

   _____

Give answers in simplest radical form if necessary.

3. The points *X*(3, 4) and *Y*(9, 1) lie on the circumference of a circle. There is exactly 60° of arc between *X* and *Y*. Find the radius of the circle.

   _____

4. Find the coordinates of all possible centers of the circle in Exercise 3.

   _____

5. Find the intersection point(s) of the circle $(x + 2)^2 + y^2 = 25$ and the line $2x + y = 3$.

   _____

6. Find the intersection point(s) of the circle $(x + 2)^2 + y^2 = 25$ and the line $y = \dfrac{4}{3}x - \dfrac{17}{3}$.

   _____

7. Describe the relationship between the circle and the line in Exercise 6.

   _____

   _____

8. Find the intersection point(s) of the circle $(x + 2)^2 + y^2 = 25$ and the circle $x^2 + y^2 = 9$.

   _____

9. Describe the relationship between the two circles in Exercise 8.

   _____

   _____

Name _____ Date _____ Class_____

Equation of a Parabola
Practice and Problem Solving: A/B

For Problems 1–2, state whether the statement is true or false.

1. The distance from any point on a parabola to the focus
   of the parabola is equal to the distance from that point
   on the parabola to the directrix of the parabola.   _____

2. In parabolas that open downward, the focus is above the
   directrix.   _____

**For Problems 3–4, write the equation of the parabola with the given
focus and directrix.**

3. Focus: $(0, 1)$; Directrix: $y = -1$ 4. Focus: $(0, -2)$; Directrix: $y = 2$

   Equation: _____   Equation: _____

**For Problems 5–6, write the equation of the parabola given the focus,
directrix, and value of p. Then graph the parabola.**

5. Focus: $(6, -2)$; Directrix: $y = -6$ 6. Focus: $(-1, 2)$; Directrix: $y = -4$

   $p = 2$ $p = 3$

   Equation: _____   Equation: _____

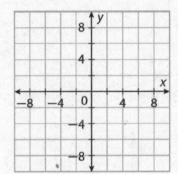   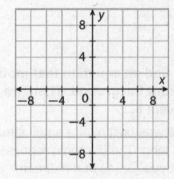

Name _____ Date _____ Class_____

LESSON 17-2

Equation of a Parabola

Practice and Problem Solving: C

For Problems 1–2, write the equation of the parabola with the given focus and directrix.

1. Focus: (0, –8); Directrix: $y = 8$

   Equation: _____

2. Focus: (0, –2); Directrix: $y = 2$

   Equation: _____

For Problems 3–4, write the equation of the parabola given the focus, directrix, and value of *p*. Then graph the parabola.

3. Focus: (5, 7); Directrix: $y = 1$

   $p = 3$

   Equation: _____

4. Focus: (4, –3); Directrix: $x = –2$

   $p = 3$

   Equation: _____

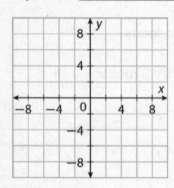

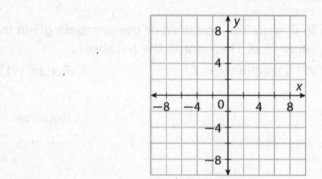

For Problem 5, find an equation that models the shape, using the *x*-axis to represent the ground. Then graph the parabola to find the answer to Problem 6.

A wooden bridge was built over a small stream. The bridge is 14 feet long. The parabola representing this shape has focus (0, –1) and a directrix of $y = 7$.

5. Equation: _____

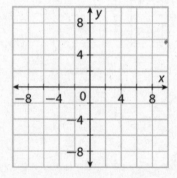

6. Which point on the shape identified the top of the bridge? What are the coordinates of this point? How tall is the bridge?

   _____

LESSON
18-1

Volume of Prisms and Cylinders

Practice and Problem Solving: A/B

Find the volume of each prism. Round to the nearest tenth if necessary.

1.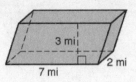

   the oblique rectangular prism

   _____

2.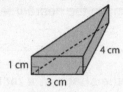

   the right triangular prism

   _____

3. a cube with edge length 0.75 m _____

Find the volume of each cylinder. Give your answers both in terms of π and rounded to the nearest tenth.

4.

   _____

5.

   _____

6. a cylinder with base circumference 18π ft and height 10 ft _____

Describe the effect of each change on the volume of the given figure.

7.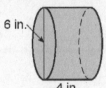

   The dimensions are halved.

   _____

8.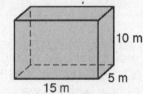

   The dimensions are divided by 5.

   _____

Find the volume of each composite figure. Round to the nearest tenth.

9.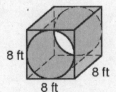

   _____

10.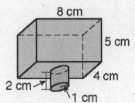

   _____

LESSON 18-1

Volume of Prisms and Cylinders

Practice and Problem Solving: C

1. Find the volume-to-side-length ratio for these two cylinders. Round to the nearest tenth.

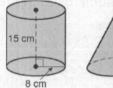

_____

A chocolate bar is in the shape of a rectangular prism with length 5 in., width $2\frac{1}{4}$ in., and height $\frac{1}{4}$ in. The bar weighs 1.75 ounces. The chart shows some of the nutritional information for the chocolate bar. Round your answers to Problems 2–4 to the nearest hundredth.

Serving size $\frac{1}{2}$ bar
Calories 135
Total fat 8 g (12% DV)
Total carb 14 g (5% DV)

2. Find the density of the chocolate bar (ounces/cubic inch).

3. Find the volume of chocolate that contains 100 calories.   _____

4. The "% DV" indicates the percentage of the recommended daily amount for that nutrient. Find the volume of chocolate that would provide 100% of the recommended daily amount of carbohydrates. (*Note:* This is NOT a healthy diet.)   _____

In the sciences, quantities of liquids are measured in liters and milliliters. One milliliter of water has the same volume as a cube with edge length 1 centimeter.

5. Tell what size cube has the same volume as 1 liter of water.

_____

6. In a science lab, liquids are often measured in tall, thin cylinders called graduated cylinders. One graduated cylinder has a diameter of 2 centimeters, and 8 milliliters of water are poured into it. Tell how high the water will reach. Round to the nearest tenth.   _____

Find the volume of each figure. Round to the nearest tenth.

7.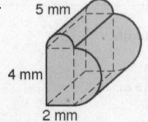

8.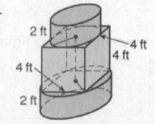

_____   _____

Name _____ Date _____ Class_____

Write each formula.

1. volume of a pyramid with base area B and height h _____

2. volume of a square pyramid with base edge s and height h _____

Find the volume of each pyramid. Round to the nearest tenth.

3.

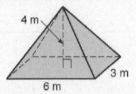

4 m
6 m
3 m

rectangular pyramid

_____

4.

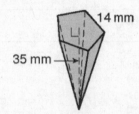

14 mm
35 mm

regular pentagonal pyramid

_____

5. a square pyramid with side length 10 in. and height 12 in. _____

6. an octagonal pyramid with base area 27 ft² and height 6 ft _____

Find the missing measure. Round to the nearest tenth.

7. Given a square pyramid with a height of 3 in. and a volume

   of 21 in., find the length of one side of the square base. _____

8. Find the height of a triangular pyramid with a volume of

   13 m³ and a base area of 7 m². _____

Find the volume of the composite figures.

9.

1 ft 5 ft
1 ft
6 ft

10.

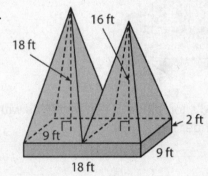

18 ft
16 ft
9 ft
2 ft
9 ft
18 ft

_____   _____

LESSON
18-2

Volume of Pyramids

Practice and Problem Solving: C

1. The figure shows a square-based pyramid with a height equal to the side length of the base. The segment connecting the top vertex to its closest corner is perpendicular to the base. Draw a net for this pyramid below. Then, using a separate sheet of paper, cut out three of these shapes. Fold them into pyramids, and assemble them into a cube. Describe what this demonstrates.

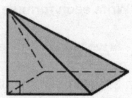

_____

_____

2. A square pyramid has a height equal to its base's side length, and its surface area is equal to its volume (although the units are different). Find the side length of the base. Give both an exact answer and an answer rounded to the nearest tenth.

_____

3. Draw a figure that has exactly two-thirds the volume of this regular hexagonal prism.

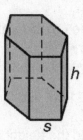

Find the volume of each figure. Round to the nearest tenth if necessary.

4.

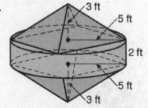

a child's top made of two pyramids with a cylinder in between

5.

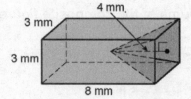

a crystal sculpture of a rectangular prism with a square pyramid carved out of one end

_____ _____

LESSON
18-3

Volume of Cones

Practice and Problem Solving: A/B

Find the volume of each cone. Give your answers both in terms of π and rounded to the nearest tenth.

1.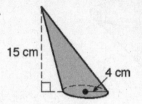

2.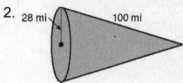

_____   _____

3.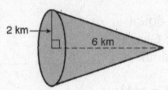

4. a cone with diameter 15 yd and height 10 yd

_____

5. a cone with base circumference 6π meters and a height equal to half the radius

_____

6. Compare the volume of a cone and the volume of a cylinder with equal height and base area.

_____

7. An ant lion is an insect that digs cone-shaped pits in loose dirt to trap ants. When an ant tumbles down into the pit, the ant lion eats it. A typical ant lion pit has a radius of 1 inch and a depth of 2 inches. Find the volume of dirt the ant lion moved to dig its hole. Round to the nearest tenth.

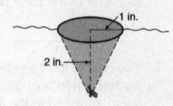

_____

Find the volume of each composite figure. Round to the nearest tenth.

8.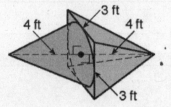

9.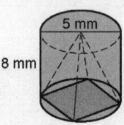

_____   _____

LESSON 18-3 Volume of Cones

Practice and Problem Solving: C

Find the volume of each figure. Round to the nearest tenth.

1.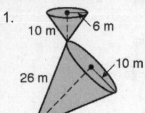

2.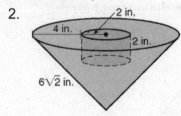

_____   _____

3. A cone has a height equal to its radius, and its surface area is equal to its volume (although the units are different). Find the radius. Give both an exact answer and an answer rounded to the nearest tenth. _____

4. A paper cone for serving roasted almonds has a volume of 406π cubic centimeters. A smaller cone has half the radius and half the height of the larger cone. What is the volume of the smaller cone? Give your answer in terms of π. _____

Use the figure of a pitcher for Problems 5 and 6. The heights given in the drawing are based on the height if the pitcher were a complete cone. Give your answers in terms of π.

5. The conic-shaped pitcher shown has 98π in^3 of liquid in it. Find the diameter of the base of the pitcher.

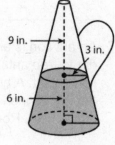

_____

6. The part of the cone that was removed to create an opening for the pitcher would hold about 2 fluid ounces. Find the number of ounces of liquid, rounded to the nearest whole ounce, that could be added to the pitcher to completely fill it. (*Hint*: 1 fl oz ≈ 1.805 in^3) Explain how you solved the problem.

_____

_____

_____

Volume of Spheres

LESSON 18-4

Practice and Problem Solving: A/B

Find each measurement. Give your answers in terms of π.

1.

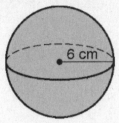

the volume of the sphere

_____

2.

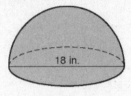

the volume of the hemisphere

_____

3. the radius of a sphere with a volume of $36,000\pi$ mm³

_____

4. Margot is thirsty after a 5-km run for charity. The organizers offer the containers of water shown in the figure. Margot wants the one with the greater volume of water. Tell which container Margot should pick.

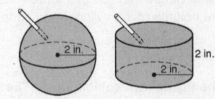

_____

Find the volume of each composite figure. Round your answers to the nearest tenth.

5.

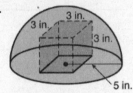

_____

6.

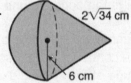

_____

7.

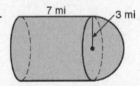

_____

8.

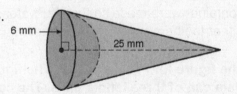

_____

9. The figure shows a grapefruit half. The radius to the outside of the rind is 5 cm. The radius to the inside of the rind is 4 cm. The edible part of the grapefruit is divided into 12 equal sections. Find the volume of the half grapefruit and the volume of one edible section. Give your answers in terms of π.

_____

LESSON 18-4

Volume of Spheres

Practice and Problem Solving: C

1. A sphere has radius *r*. Draw a composite figure made up of a square prism (not a cube) and a square pyramid that has the same volume as the sphere.

2. Find the surface area of the composite figure you drew in Problem 1. The formula for the surface area of a sphere is $4\pi r^2$.

   _____

3. Consider a composite figure made up of a cylinder and a cone of the same height that has the same volume as a sphere with radius *r*. Find the heights of the cylinder and cone.

   _____

Use the figure for Problems 4–6. The figure shows a hollow, sealed container with some water inside.

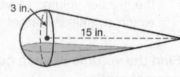

4. There is just enough water in the container to exactly fill the hemisphere. The container is held so that the point of the cone is down and the altitude of the cone is exactly vertical. Find the height of the water in the cone. Round to the nearest tenth.

   _____

5. Suppose the amount of water in the container is exactly enough to fill the cone. The container is held so that the hemisphere is down and the altitude of the cone is exactly vertical. Find the height of the water in the container. Round to the nearest tenth.

   _____

6. Find the height of the cone with the same radius if the container were made so that the water would exactly fill either the hemisphere or the cone.

   _____

Use the figure for Problems 7–9. The figure shows a can of three tennis balls. The can is just large enough so that the tennis balls will fit inside with the lid on. The diameter of each tennis ball is 2.5 in. Give exact fraction answers.

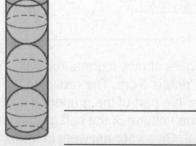

7. Find the total volume of the can.   _____

8. Find the volume of empty space inside the can.   _____

9. Tell what percent of the can is occupied by the tennis balls.   _____

Name _____ Date _____ Class_____

LESSON 19-1

Cross Sections and Solids of Rotation

Practice and Problem Solving: A/B

**For Problems 1–6, tell what kind of solid can be made from each net.
If there is no solid that can be made from the given net, write "none."**

1.

   _____

2.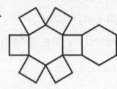

   _____

3.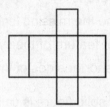

   _____

4.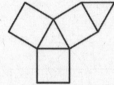

   _____

5.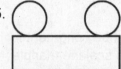

   _____

6.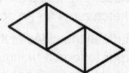

   _____

**For Problems 7–13, name the shape of the cross section
produced by slicing each of these solids as described.**

7. Vertical cross section of a cylinder _____

8. Horizontal cross section of a cylinder _____

9. Cross section of a sphere not through the diameter _____

10. Horizontal cross section of a square pyramid _____

11. Vertical cross section of a square pyramid through the top

    vertex _____

12. Vertical cross section of a square pyramid not through the

    top vertex _____

13. Horizontal cross section of a rectangular prism _____

14. What can be said about the shape of a cross section that is parallel
    to the base of a solid? _____

**Describe how to generate each 3-dimensional figure by rotating a
2-dimensional figure around a line.**

15. Cone _____

16. Sphere _____

17. Cylinder _____

LESSON 19-1

Cross Sections and Solids of Rotation

Practice and Problem Solving: C

To solve Problems 1–3, think about how nets can be used to form solid figures.

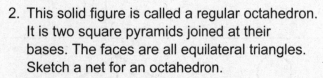

1. Name the missing length for this net of a cylinder. _____

   What feature of the cylinder is determined by the length of

   the shorter sides of the rectangle? _____

2. This solid figure is called a regular octahedron. It is two square pyramids joined at their bases. The faces are all equilateral triangles. Sketch a net for an octahedron.

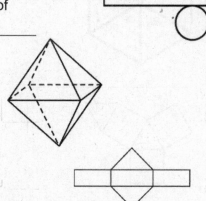

3. Mark all the sides of this net that must be congruent in order to form a triangular prism with a scalene triangle base. For sides that do not *have* to be congruent, use a different number of slash marks.

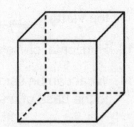

Think about the properties of 3-dimensional figures to solve Problems 4–10.

4. Name the two possible geometric figures that can result from the

   intersection of a plane and a sphere. _____

5. A square pyramid is intersected by a plane at a 45° angle from horizontal. What shape is the cross section? _____

6. A plane that intersects a cylinder horizontally creates a circular cross section. If the plane intersects the cylinder at an angle, what shape is

   the cross section? _____

7. If a plane intersects a cube at an angle so as to slice off one of its

   corners, what shape is the cross section? _____

8. If a plane intersects a 1-inch cube at a 45° angle through opposite edges, what are the dimensions of the cross section?

   _____

9. Sketch a plane intersecting the cube to create a hexagon.

10. Sketch a figure that could be rotated around this line to create a torus (donut shape).

LESSON 19-2

Surface Area of Prisms and Cylinders
Practice and Problem Solving: A/B

For Problems 1–6, find the surface area of each solid figure. For Problems 1–4, write the measures of the solid figures on the corresponding parts of their nets. For cylinders, give answers in terms of π.

1. Cube: _____ units²

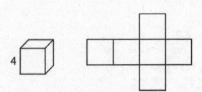

2. Cylinder: _____ units²

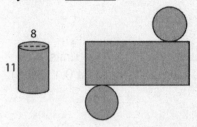

3. Rectangular prism: _____ units²

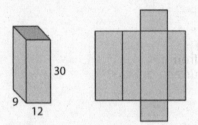

4. Triangular prism: _____ units²
   Height of base = 25 units

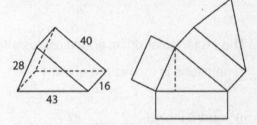

5. Cylinder: _____ units²

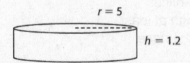

6. Triangular prism: _____ units²

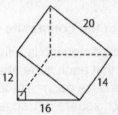

For Problems 7 and 8, find the surface area of each composite figure. Show your work.

7. Cylinder on top of rectangular prism

   _____ units²

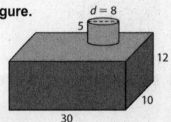

8. 5-inch cube with 2-inch cylinder removed

   _____ units²

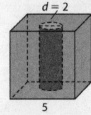

LESSON
19-2
Surface Area of Prisms and Cylinders
Practice and Problem Solving: C

Find the surface area of each figure. Show your work.
For Problems 1–3, sketch a net of the figure.

1. Cylinder whose diameter is

   equal to its height _____ units²

2. Triangular prism _____ units²
   (Round lengths to nearest 0.1 units.)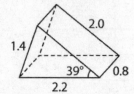

3. Rectangular prism _____ cm²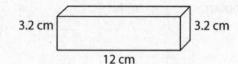

4. The rectangular prism above represents a stick of butter. The

   dimensions in inches are about $1\frac{1}{4} \times 1\frac{1}{4} \times 4\frac{3}{4}$. Find the surface area

   in square inches. _____ in²

   Multiply your answer by 6.45 to get the
   approximate equivalent in square centimeters. _____ cm² .

Find the surface area of the composite shapes.

5. A three-dimensional pentomino is a figure formed by five identical
   cubes arranged so that each cube shares a common face with at least
   one other cube. Visualize each pentomino in 3D and find its surface
   area, given that each square is 1 square unit.

   _____

6. Find the surface area of the cube with a cylinder removed.

   _____ cm²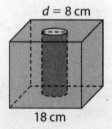

Name _____ Date _____ Class_____

Surface Area of Pyramids and Cones
Practice and Problem Solving: A/B

For Problems 1–4, find the surface area of each part of the solid figure.
Add to find the total surface area. For cones, give answers in terms of π.

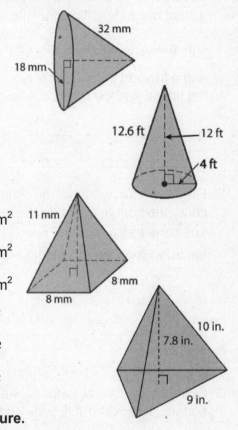

1. What is the base area of the cone?   _____ mm²

   What is the lateral surface area?   _____ mm²

   What is the total surface area?   _____ mm²

2. What is the base area of the cone?   _____ ft²

   What is the lateral surface area?   _____ ft²

   What is the total surface area?   _____ ft²

3. What is the base area of the pyramid?   _____ mm²

   What is the lateral surface area?   _____ mm²

   What is the total surface area?   _____ mm²

4. What is the base area of the pyramid?   _____ in²

   What is the lateral surface area?   _____ in²

   What is the total surface area?   _____ in²

For Problems 5 and 6, find the surface area of each figure.

5. _____ in²

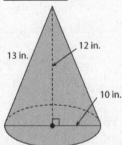

6. _____ cm²

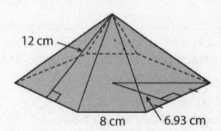

For Problems 7 and 8, find the surface area of each composite figure.

7. _____ m²

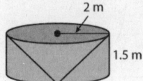

8. _____ cm²

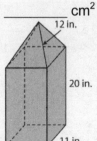

LESSON
19-3

Surface Area of Pyramids and Cones

Practice and Problem Solving: C

Find the surface area of each figure. Show your work.

1. The square pyramid to the right has a base length of b and a slant height of ℓ. The gray plane is parallel to the base and cuts the pyramid into a smaller pyramid above with base $\dfrac{b}{2}$ and a frustum below. Show two different ways to calculate the lateral surface area of the frustum.

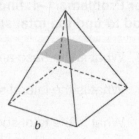

_____

_____

2. Find the surface area of the cone and then of the truncated cone (the bottom part after the top is sliced off by the plane). The cone has a radius of r and slant height of ℓ. The height of the truncated cone is half the height of the cone.

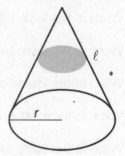

_____

_____

3. Compare the lateral surface area of the big cone with the lateral surface area of the little cone and of the truncated cone.

_____

_____

Find the surface area of the composite shapes. Show your work.

4. Square pyramid inside a cone
   side of square base = 6 cm
   slant height of pyramid = 5 cm
   slant height of cone = 5.8 cm

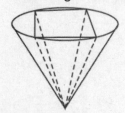

5. Double cone
   radius of base: 12
   height of left cone: 16
   height of right cone: 5

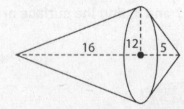

_____   _____

LESSON 19-4

Surface Area of Spheres

Practice and Problem Solving: A/B

Solve Problems 1–8 about the surface area of spheres.
Give surface areas in terms of π.

1. Surface area = _____ mi²

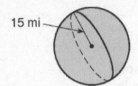

15 mi

2. Surface area = _____ m²

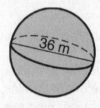

36 m

18 in.

3. What is the total surface area of the hemisphere? _____ in²
   Show your work.

4. If the radius of the grapefruit is 5 centimeters, what is the surface area

   of the half grapefruit? _____ cm² Show your work.

5. If you double the length, width, and height of a rectangular prism, what

   happens to the surface area? _____

   If you double the radius of a sphere, what happens to the surface area?

   _____

   Write equations to prove your answer.

   _____

6. In the case of the prism, you doubled three dimensions. In the
   case of the sphere, you doubled just the radius. Why do you
   get the same results?

   _____

Find the surface area of each composite figure. Show your work.

7. _____ mm²

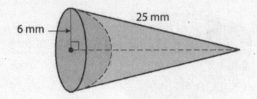

6 mm   25 mm

8. _____ in²

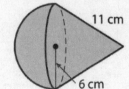

11 cm

6 cm

LESSON 19-4

Surface Area of Spheres
Practice and Problem Solving: C

Find the surface areas of the given figures in terms of π. Show your work in the space to the right.

1. The volume of a sphere is given by the formula $V = \frac{4}{3}\pi r^3$. What is the

   surface area of a sphere whose volume is $\frac{256\pi}{3}$ yd³? _____ yd²

2. Ganymede, one of Jupiter's moons, is the largest moon in the solar system, with a radius of 1640 miles. The radius of Earth's moon is approximately 1080 miles. Find the surface area of each. About how many times as great is the surface area of Ganymede as the surface area of Earth's moon? Compare the ratio of their surface areas to the ratio of their radii.

   Ganymede: _____ mi²   Moon: _____ mi²

   Ratio of surface areas: _____   Ratio of radii: _____

3. What is the surface area of a sphere with a
   great circle whose area is 225π cm²? _____ cm²

   Make a general statement about the surface area of a sphere and the area of its great circle.

   _____

4. The three tennis balls just fit in this can with the lid on. Find the surface area of the can and of the three balls in terms of π and the radius r.

   SA of can _____ in²   *SA* of 3 balls _____ in²

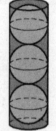

5. In Problem 4, what do you notice about the surface area of a sphere and the lateral surface area of a cylinder with the same radius?

   _____

Find the surface area of each composite figure. Show your work.

6. _____ in²   7. _____ ft²

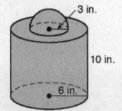

3 in.

10 in.

6 in.

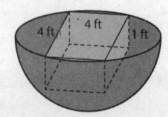

4 ft

4 ft

4 ft

1 ft

LESSON 20-1

Scale Factor

Practice and Problem Solving: A/B

In Problems 1–3, state how each transformation affects the area.

1. The base of a parallelogram is multiplied by $\frac{3}{4}$.

   _____

2. A rectangle has length 12 yd and width 11 yd. The length is divided by 6.

   _____

3. A triangle has vertices $A(2, 3)$, $B(5, 2)$, and $C(5, 4)$. The transformation is $(x, y) \rightarrow (x, 2y)$.

   _____

In Problems 4–6, state how each transformation affects the perimeter or circumference and area.

4. The length and width of the rectangle are multiplied by $\frac{4}{3}$.

   _____

5. A triangle has base 1.5 m and height 6 m. Both base and height are tripled.

   _____

6. A circle with radius 2 has center (2, 2). The transformation is $(x, y) \rightarrow \left(\frac{1}{2}x, \frac{1}{2}y\right)$.

   _____

In Problems 7 and 8, state how each transformation affects the surface area and volume.

7. The dimensions of a rectangular prism are multiplied by a scale factor of 2.

   _____

8. The dimensions of a right cylinder are multiplied by a scale factor of $\frac{1}{2}$.

   _____

Scale Factor

Practice and Problem Solving: C

Irene has learned how to solve problems about the effects of changing dimensions, but she is suspicious about math formulas until she has seen a proof. Complete Problems 1 and 2 to assuage Irene's doubts. Use A_i to indicate the initial area and A_c to indicate the changed area.

1. Show that multiplying the base and the height of a triangle by n multiplies the area by n^2.

   _____

   _____

   _____

2. Show that multiplying the radius of a circle by n multiplies the area by n^2.

   _____

   _____

   _____

For Problems 3–5, assume the resulting figure is similar to the original. Give answers in simplest radical form.

3. The area of a circle with radius 9 ft is multiplied by $\dfrac{5}{2}$.

   Find the length of the radius of the resulting circle.   _____

4. The area of a square with diagonals $\sqrt{2}$ in. long is doubled.
   Find the length of a side of the resulting square.   _____

5. The area of a circle with a radius of $\sqrt{3}$ cm is squared.
   Find the length of the radius of the resulting circle.   _____

The volume of a rectangular prism can be found with the formula $V = \ell wh$, in which V is the volume, ℓ is the length, w is the width, and h is the height.

6. Describe the effect on the volume of multiplying
   the height of a rectangular prism by 5.   _____

7. Describe the effect on the volume of multiplying
   the length, the width, and the height of a
   rectangular prism by 2.   _____

8. The volume of a rectangular prism is divided
   by 343 without changing the ratios among the
   length, width, and height. Describe the effect
   of the volume change on the height.   _____

LESSON 20-2

Modeling and Density

Practice and Problem Solving: A/B

In Problems 1–3, find the population density.

1. Park rangers counted 7 coyotes over an area of 25 square miles.

   _____

2. A major metropolitan city has an average of 60,000 people visiting the city's park during peak hours. The city park is 3.41 km².

   _____

3. About 50,000 full-grown Canadian geese were estimated to live in the state of Minnesota in 1990. The state of Minnesota is about 86,000 square miles.

   _____

In Problems 4–6, state how the following changes will affect the population density.

4. Park rangers counted 7 coyotes over an area of 25 square miles. One of the coyotes left the pack and is no longer in the area.

   _____

5. A major metropolitan city has an average of 60,000 people visit the city's park during peak hours. The city park is 3.41 km². An outdoor concert is planned in the park and 40,000 additional people are expected to attend the concert.

   _____

6. About 50,000 full-grown Canadian geese were estimated to live in the state of Minnesota in 1990. The state of Minnesota is about 86,000 square miles. It is estimated that 62,000 goslings were produced and will become full-grown adults in 1991.

   _____

Find the population density.

7. Cardton City has a population of 2046. Its border can be modeled by a rectangle with vertices $A(-1, 1)$, $B(1, 1)$, $C(1, 0)$, and $D(-1, 0)$, where each unit on the coordinate plane represents 1 mile. Find the approximate population density of Cardton City.

LESSON 20-2

Modeling and Density

Practice and Problem Solving: C

For Problems 1–4, use the information below to answer the population density questions.

On a range of 250 acres, there was a total of 960 rabbits. During the following year studies indicate the rates for this population:

Birthrate – 2925/yr   Moving into range – 125/yr
Mortality – 1530/yr   Moving out of range – 550/yr

1. What was the population density at the beginning of the study?

   _____

2. Is the population of rabbits increasing or decreasing each year based on the studies?

   _____

3. Calculate the population density at the end of the first year.

   _____

4. A large number of people start setting out traps for the rabbits. What is likely to happen to the population density with this change?

   _____

For Problems 5–8, use the information below to answer the population density questions.

On September 1, 2005, at the beginning of the squirrel-hunting season, biologists counted 85 red squirrels in a 25-acre forest. On December 1, 2005, 32 red squirrels were counted in the forest.

5. What was the density of the red squirrel population on September 1, 2005?

   _____

6. What was the density of the red squirrel population on December 15, 2005?

   _____

7. What factors could have affected the density of the population between September 1, 2005 and December 15, 2005?

   _____

   _____

LESSON 20-3

Problem Solving with Constraints
Practice and Problem Solving: A/B

In Problems 1–4, solve for the missing dimension of the figure.

1. A rectangular prism has a volume of 432 cubic feet. Two of the dimensions of the rectangular prism are the same measure. The other dimension is equal to the sum of the other two dimensions. What are the prism's dimensions?

   _____

2. A cone's height is six times greater than the measure of the cone's radius. The volume of the cylinder is 169.56 in^3. What are the cone's dimensions? Use 3.14 for π.

   _____

3. A cube has a volume of 343 cubic centimeters. The length, width, and the height of the figure are equal. What are the cube's dimensions?

   _____

4. A circle has an area of 530.66 square inches. What is the circle's radius? Use 3.14 for π.

   _____

In Problems 5–7, solve the problems using the information provided.

5. The height of a cylindrical can is 2.25 inches greater than the measure of the can's diameter. The volume of the cylinder is 52.18 in^3. What are the can's dimensions? Use 3.14 for π.

   _____

6. A tennis court in the shape of a rectangle has an area of 7200 square feet. One pair of sides measures twice the length of the other pair of sides. What are the dimensions of the tennis court?

   _____

7. A fountain is in the shape of a right triangle. The area of the fountain is 12 square meters. One leg of the triangle measures one and a half times the length of the other leg. What are the lengths of all three sides of the fountain?

   _____

Name _____ Date _____ Class_____

 # Problem Solving with Constraints
Practice and Problem Solving: C

In Problems 1–6, solve for the missing information.

1. The diameter of a cylindrical water tank is half the measure of the cylinder's height. The tank has a volume of 1570 cubic feet. Find the height of the tank. Use 3.14 for π.

   _____

2. The height of a bookcase is $2\frac{1}{2}$ times the width. The depth is $\frac{1}{3}$ of the width. The volume of the cabinet is 22,500 in^3. What are the bookshelf's dimensions?

   _____

3. Concrete costs $105 per cubic yard. Alice is making a rectangular patio measuring 20 feet long by 16 feet wide. The cost of the concrete for her patio floor is $622.22. How thick is the patio floor (rounded to the nearest inch)?

   _____

4. A swimming pool in the shape of a rectangular prism has a bottom, no top, two square sides, and two rectangular sides with a length equal to twice the length of the square sides. All four sides share a common height. The total area of the five sides is 288 ft^2. Find the volume of the swimming pool.

   _____

5. Sean's filing cabinet is 1 foot wide and 3 feet high. The folders that he keeps in the file cabinet are 12 inches wide, 1 inch thick, and 9 inches tall. The file cabinet can hold 144 of these folders. How deep is the file cabinet?

   _____

6. A 5-foot-tall cylindrical container with a diameter of 6 inches is filled with a gas that costs $60 per cubic foot. What is the total value of the gas in the container if it is filled completely?

   _____

LESSON 21-1 Probability and Set Theory

Practice and Problem Solving: A/B

For Problems 1–6, write each statement in set notation. Use the descriptions of the sets to the right to complete each statement.

1. the intersection of sets *A* and *B*

   _____

2. the complement of set *A*

   _____

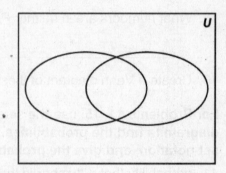

A = {21, 23, 25, 27, 29}

B = {21, 24, 27, 30}

U = {20, 21, 22, 23, 24, 25, 26, 27, 28, 29, 30}

3. the union of sets *A* and *B* _____

4. the complement of set *B* _____

5. the number of elements in set *A* _____

6. the number of elements in set *B* _____

7. Define set *C* so that *C* is a subset of set *A*. _____

8. Define set *D* so that *D* is a subset of set *B*. _____

For Problems 9 and 10, use the descriptions of the sets in the box above.

9. Create a Venn diagram to represent sets *A, B,* and *U*.

10. Describe the parts of the Venn diagram that correspond to 1–4 above.

    1) _____

    2) _____

    3) _____

    4) _____

Refer to the descriptions of the sets above and the Venn diagram to find the probabilities in Problems 11–14.

11. Use set notation to write a fraction giving the probability that a number chosen from the universal set will be in set *A*. Fill in the numbers.

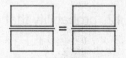

12. What is the probability that a number in *U* is *not* in *A*? _____

13. What is the probability that a number in *U* is in $A \cup B$? _____

14. What is the probability that a number in *U* is *not* in *A* or *B*? _____

**LESSON
21-1**

Probability and Set Theory

Practice and Problem Solving: C

**For Problems 1–7, the universal set consists of the natural numbers
from 1 to 20. For each description, write a statement in set notation.**

1. Set *P* _____

2. Set *T* _____

3. Set *F* _____

> Set *U*: integers from 1 to 20
> Set *P*: prime numbers
> Set *T*: multiples of 3
> Set *F*: multiples of 5

4. number of elements in set *P* _____

5. intersection of sets *P* and *T* _____

6. union of sets *T* and *F* _____

7. complement of set *P* _____

Use the sets above to solve Problems 8–10.

8. Explain why the intersection of all three sets,
   P, T, and *F,* is the empty set.

   _____

   _____

9. What numbers are in neither *P, T,* nor *F*?

   _____

10. Create a Venn diagram of these sets.

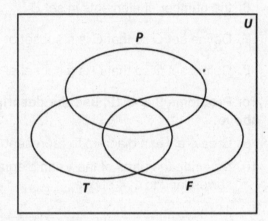

**For Problems 11–15, use the sets defined above and your Venn
diagram to find the probabilities. Write each probability statement in
set notation, and give the probabilities in simplest form.**

11. probability that a number in the universal set is a multiple of 3

    _____

12. probability that a number in the universal set is *not* a multiple of 3

    _____

13. What is $P(T) + P(\sim T)$? _____

14. probability that a number in the universal set is a multiple of *both* 3 and 5

    _____

15. probability that a number in the universal set is prime or a multiple of 5

    _____

LESSON
21-2

Permutations and Probability

Practice and Problem Solving: A/B

For Problems 1–8, give the value of each expression.

1. 5! = _____

2. 6! = _____

3. 7! = _____

4. $\dfrac{6!}{5!}$ = _____

5. $\dfrac{7!}{6!}$ = _____

6. $\dfrac{8!}{7!}$ = _____

7. Suppose n stands for any number. Write a fraction to show n factorial

   divided by $(n-1)$ factorial. Find its value. _____

8. What is the value of $\dfrac{n!}{(n-2)!}$? _____

Use the Fundamental Counting Principle to solve Problems 9–11.

9. Alicia is designing a flag with 3 stripes. She has 5 different colors of fabric to use in any order she likes, but she does not want 2 stripes next to each other to be the same color. How many different color patterns can she choose from? Explain your answer. _____

10. A travel agent is offering a vacation package. Participants choose the type of tour, a meal plan, and a hotel class from the chart to the right. How many different vacation packages

    are offered? _____

Tour	Meal	Hotel
Walking	Restaurant	4-Star
Boat	Picnic	3-Star
Bicycle		2-Star
		1-Star

11. There are 8 marbles in a bag, all of different colors. In how many orders can 4 marbles be chosen? _____

For Problems 12–14, find the probabilities.

12. Gil's padlock can be opened by entering 3 digits in the right order (digits can be repeated). How many different orders of digits are there? What is the probability that someone could guess the right order on the first try?

    _____

    _____

13. A playlist includes 8 songs, including Kim's favorite and second favorite. How many different ways can the playlist be shuffled? What is the probability that Kim's favorite song will be first and her second favorite song will be second? Explain your answers.

    _____

    _____

    _____

14. What is the probability that a family with 4 children will have all girls? _____

LESSON 21-2 Permutations and Probability

Practice and Problem Solving: C

For Problems 1–4, evaluate each expression.

1. $\dfrac{7! - 4!}{(6-3)!}$ = _____

2. $\dfrac{6!}{3!(8-5)!}$ = _____

3. $\dfrac{5!\,4!}{9!}$ = _____

4. $\dfrac{11!}{6!\,5!}$ = _____

For Problems 5–9, find the number of permutations.

5. A 10-person board of trustees is choosing a chairperson, a secretary, and a publicist. If they have already decided upon a chairperson, in how many ways can they choose a secretary and a publicist? _____

6. The door code to gain access to a top-secret laboratory is 6 digits. The first 3 digits of the code are all odd, and the last 3 digits are all even. Digits can be used more than once. How many possible codes are there? _____

7. Find the number of different permutations of the letters in the word INVISIBILITY. _____

8. How many ways can the letters from *A* through *H* be used to create 5-letter passwords if there are no repeated letters? _____

9. The 13 diamonds from a deck of cards are shuffled and laid out in a row. How many arrangements are possible if the first card is the ace? If the first card is a face card (J, Q, K)? Explain your answers. _____

For Problems 10–12, find the probabilities.

10. Miguel is trying to remember Aerin's phone number. He knows that the last 4 digits include a 3, a 7, and two 6s, but he's not sure about the order. What is the probability that he will guess correctly? _____

11. Fran needs to create an 8-character password with any combination of digits and/or letters. What is the probability that her password will be identical to someone else's? (Write your answer in exponential form.) _____

12. Charlene and Amir are scrambling the letters in words to play a word game. What is the probability that they will scramble the word LANGUAGE the same way? _____

LESSON 21-3

Combinations and Probability

Practice and Problem Solving: A/B

Use the scenario in the box for Problems 1–4.

> Calvin has enough money to get 3 new T-shirts at a buy two, get one free sale. There are 8 color choices, and he wants to get 3 different colors. How many possible combinations of 3 colors are there?

1. Explain why you should use combinations rather than permutations for this problem.

   _____

2. Tell what the variables n and r stand for in the combinations formula, $_nC_r = \dfrac{n!}{r!(n-r)!}$, and identify their values for this problem.

   n _____ r _____

3. Substitute the values of n and r into the formula and solve to find the number of combinations of 3 T-shirts. _____

4. The formula for combinations is equal to the formula for permutations divided by $r!$ Explain how dividing by $r!$ relates to this problem.

   _____

   _____

5. Find the number of combinations of 7 objects taken 4 at a time. _____

6. Rachel has 10 valuable baseball cards. She wants to select 2 of them to sell online. How many different combinations of 2 cards could she choose? _____

7. If Rachel picked the cards at random, what is the probability that one of the 2 cards would be her Ken Griffey, Jr., card? Explain your answer. _____

   _____

8. Mrs. Marshall has 11 boys and 14 girls in her kindergarten class. In how many ways can she select 2 boys to pass out a snack? _____

9. In how many ways can Mrs. Marshall select 3 students to carry papers to the office? Show your calculations. _____

10. What is the probability that Adam will be one of the students chosen to carry papers to the office? _____

Combinations and Probability

Practice and Problem Solving: C

LESSON 21-3

For Problems 1–3, calculate the number of combinations.

1. For English class you are required to read 4 books out of a list of
   20 books. How many 4-book combinations are there? _____
   One of the books is *To Kill a Mockingbird.* How many of the
   combinations include this book? _____

   What fraction of the total combinations include any particular book? _____

2. Rick & Jean's ice cream shop has 18 flavors of ice cream. How many
   3-scoop combinations are possible if the same flavor can be used for
   more than 1 scoop? _____

3. Bree has to select 5 photos from a box containing 25 photos to use in
   the yearbook. How many different sets of 5 photos could she choose? _____

For Problems 4–8, calculate the probabilities.

4. Jordan wants to turn on 3 lights, but he's not sure which of the
   5 switches on the panel control the lights. What is the probability
   that he will guess the correct 3 switches? _____

   What is the probability that he will guess at least one wrong switch? _____

5. Four friends are playing a card game that uses
   16 cards—the jack, queen, king, and ace of each
   of the 4 suits. The cards are dealt out, each
   person receiving 4 cards. What is the probability
   that one person will get all 4 aces?

   Explain. _____

Clubs	Diamonds	Hearts	Spades
♣	♦	♥	♠

   _____

6. In the scenario for Problem 5, what is the probability that one person
   will get jack, queen, king, and ace of one suit? _____

7. What is the probability that one person will get jack, queen, king, and
   ace of any suits? Explain.

   _____

   _____

8. Garrett is playing a game with a spinner that has the numbers 1–6.
   He has 3 spins left, and he needs at least two 6s in order to win.
   What are his chances of winning? Explain.

   _____

   _____

Mutually Exclusive and Overlapping Events

LESSON 21-4

Practice and Problem Solving: A/B

For Problems 1–3, answer the questions about mutually exclusive or overlapping events.

1. Are the events "choosing a black card" and "choosing a 10" from a deck of playing cards mutually exclusive? Explain why or why not.

_____

2. If there are 52 cards in a deck, with 2 red suits (groups of 13 different cards) and 2 black suits, what is the probability that a card drawn will be black and a 10? _____

3. A can of vegetables with no label has a $\frac{1}{8}$ chance of being green beans and a $\frac{1}{5}$ chance of being corn. Are the events "green beans" and "corn" mutually exclusive? _____

   What is the probability that an unlabeled can of vegetables is either green beans or corn? _____

Ben spins a spinner with the numbers 1–8. For Problems 4–6, find each probability.

4. Ben spins a multiple of 3 or a multiple of 5. _____

5. Ben spins a number greater than 2 or an even number. _____

6. Ben spins a prime number or an odd number. _____

For Problems 7–10, use the scenario described below.

Of the 400 doctors who attended a conference, 240 practiced family medicine and 130 were from countries outside the United States. One-third of the family medicine practitioners were not from the United States.

	Family Medicine	Not Family Medicine	Total
From US	160		
Not From US		50	
Total			400

7. Complete the two-way table using this information.

8. What is the probability that a doctor at the conference practices family medicine or is from the United States? _____

9. What is the probability that a doctor at the conference practices family medicine or is not from the United States? _____

10. What is the probability that a doctor at the conference does not practice family medicine or is from the United States? _____

LESSON 21-4 Mutually Exclusive and Overlapping Events

Practice and Problem Solving: C

Use the scenario in the box for Problems 1–3. Tell whether the events are mutually exclusive (ME) or overlapping (O), and give the probability of each.

> Cards numbered 1–25 are placed in a bag and one is drawn at random.

1. drawing an odd number or a multiple of 7 _____ $P =$ _____

2. drawing an even number or a perfect square _____ $P =$ _____

3. drawing a prime number greater than 10 or a multiple of 5 _____ $P =$ _____

Use the table and description of the experiment for Problems 4–6. Express probabilities as fractions and as decimals to the nearest hundredth.

> A drug company is testing the side effects of different doses of a new drug on three different groups of volunteers.

Group	Volunteers	Daily Amount (mg)
A	353	150
B	467	200
C	310	250

4. If a volunteer is chosen randomly, what is the probability that this person receives the highest dose of the drug per day? _____

5. If a volunteer is chosen randomly, what is the probability that this person receives more than 150 milligrams per day? _____

6. If a volunteer is chosen randomly, what is the probability that this person does **not** receive 200 milligrams per day? _____

Use the scenario in the box for Problems 7 and 8. Express probabilities as decimals. Round to the nearest hundredth.

> Mr. Rodney has 28 students in his class. Six students have blonde hair, 10 have blue eyes, and 5 have brown eyes. The blonde-haired students make up $\frac{1}{5}$ of the blue-eyed students and $\frac{3}{5}$ of the brown-eyed students.

7. What is the probability that a student in the class has blonde hair and blue eyes? _____

8. What is the probability that a student in the class has blonde hair and brown eyes? _____

Find the probabilities for Problems 9 and 10. Round to the nearest hundredth.

9. A student is collecting a population of laboratory mice to be used in an experiment. He finds that of the 236 mice in the lab, 173 mice are female and 99 have pink eyes. Just 10 of the pink-eyed mice are male What is the probability that a mouse is female or has pink eyes? _____

10. A group of 4 friends buys a CD of 12 computer screen savers. Each friend will pick 1 screen saver to use on their computer. What is the probability that at least 2 of the friends will choose the same screen saver for their computer? _____

Name _____ Date _____ Class _____

Conditional Probability
Practice and Problem Solving: A/B

Use the table to find the probabilities in Problems 1–4. Write your answer as a percentage rounded to an integer.

The table shows the results of a customer satisfaction survey of 100 randomly selected shoppers at a mall. They were asked if they would shop at an earlier time if the mall opened earlier.

	Ages 10–20	Ages 21–45	Ages 46–65	65 and Older	Total
Yes	0.13	0.02	0.08	0.24	0.47
No	0.25	0.10	0.15	0.03	0.53
Total	0.38	0.12	0.23	0.27	1

1. What is the probability that a person aged 10–20 answered yes?

   _____

2. What is the probability that a person aged 65 and older answered no?

   _____

3. What is the probability that a person who answered no is aged 21–45?

   _____

4. What is the probability that a person aged 46–65 answered yes?

   _____

Find each probability. Express your answer as a percentage rounded to an integer.

5. Jerrod collected data on 100 randomly selected students. He found that 62 students owned an MP3 player, and 28 of these students also owned a smartphone. What is the probability that a person who owns an MP3 player also owns a smartphone?

   _____

6. A poll of 75 students in a class shows that 61 like chocolate ice cream. Of these, 14 also like strawberry ice cream. What is the probability that a student who likes chocolate ice cream also likes strawberry ice cream?

   _____

Conditional Probability

LESSON 22-1

Practice and Problem Solving: C

Use the table to find the probabilities in Problems 1–4. Write your answer as a percentage rounded to an integer.

The table shows the results of a poll of randomly selected high school students. They were asked if they think smartphones should be allowed in class.

	9th Graders	10th Graders	11th Graders	12th Graders	Total
Yes	0.15	0.16	0.19	0.18	0.68
No	0.12	0.11	0.05	0.04	0.32
Total	0.27	0.27	0.24	0.22	1

1. What is the probability that a 9th or 10th grader answered yes?

2. What is the probability that an 11th or 12th grader answered no?

3. What is the probability that a 9th or 11th grader answered yes?

4. What is the probability that a 10th or 12th grader answered no?

Solve.

5. Sarah asked 30 randomly selected students at her high school whether they were planning to go to college and whether they were planning to move out of their parents' or guardians' homes right after high school. The results are summarized in the table.

		Go to College		
		Yes	**No**	**Total**
Move Out	**Yes**	12	9	21
	No	8	1	9

Which is more likely, that a student planning to go to college is also planning to move out, or that a student planning to move out is also planning to go to college? Justify your response with conditional probabilities.

_____

_____

Name _____ Date _____ Class_____

LESSON 22-2

Independent Events

Practice and Problem Solving: A/B

Find each probability.

1. Salene rolls a 1–6 number cube two times. What is the probability she will roll a 6 both times?

   _____

2. Kalie rolls a 1–6 number cube two times. What is the probability she will roll an even number both times?

   _____

3. Jamar rolls a 1–6 number cube three times. What is the probability he will roll an even number, then a 6, then a 4?

   _____

A bag contains 4 red balls, 6 green balls, and 8 yellow balls. Find each probability for randomly removing balls with replacement.

4. removing a yellow ball two times and then a red ball

   _____

5. removing a green ball, then a red ball, and then a yellow ball

   _____

6. removing a green ball, then a yellow ball, then a red ball, and then a green ball

   _____

For Problems 7–9, find the probability of making the spins.

7. spinning a number followed by a letter

   _____

8. spinning a 2, then a letter, then an even number

   _____

9. spinning a letter, then an odd number, then a 4

   _____

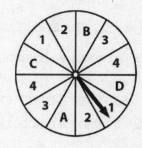

10. spinning a letter, then a 4, then a C

    _____

LESSON 22-2

Independent Events

Practice and Problem Solving: C

Find each probability.

1. In cooking class, students randomly choose 1 of 5 different recipes. Two students choose the same recipe.   _____

2. Steven rolls a 1–6 number cube four times. The result is 4 odd numbers.   _____

3. Beth draws four cards out of a 52-card deck with replacement. The deck has four aces. She randomly draws an ace four times.   _____

A bag contains 4 red balls, 2 green balls, 3 yellow balls, and 5 blue balls. Find each probability for randomly removing balls with replacement.

4. removing a yellow, a red, a green, and a blue ball   _____

5. removing a blue, a green, a green, and a yellow ball   _____

6. removing a red, a red, a yellow, and a yellow ball   _____

7. removing a green, a yellow, a yellow, and a red ball   _____

Find each probability.

8. spinning a number greater than 3 and a number less than 5

   _____

9. spinning an even number and a number greater than 4

   _____

10. spinning a number less than 3 and a number greater than 3

   _____

11. spinning an odd number and a number less than 4

   _____

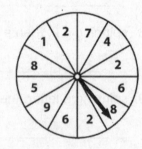

LESSON 22-3

Dependent Events

Practice and Problem Solving: A/B

A bag contains tiles with the letters shown at the right. Find the probability for randomly drawing tiles, one after the other, without replacing them.

1. A and then B   _____

2. C and then E   _____

3. B and then D   _____

4. E, then C, and then B   _____

5. D, then A, and then A   _____

A	A	A	B
B	C	C	D
E	F	G	G

There are 3 apples, 4 oranges, and a pear in a bag. Determine each probability.

6. You select an orange and then a pear at random without replacement.

_____

7. You select an apple and then a pear at random without replacement.

_____

8. You select an orange, then an apple, and then a pear at random without replacement.

_____

9. You select an apple, then an orange, and then another apple without replacement.

_____

A bag contains balls with the colors shown at the right. Find the probability for randomly selecting balls, one after the other, without replacing them.

10. blue and then red   _____

11. blue and then blue   _____

12. green and then blue   _____

13. blue and then red   _____

14. red and then red   _____

15. green and then green   _____

(green) (green) (red)
(red) (red) (red)
(blue) (blue) (blue)

Name _____ Date _____ Class_____

LESSON 22-3

Dependent Events

Practice and Problem Solving: C

The spinner shown here is spun twice.

1. The sum of the results is equal to or greater than 10, and the first spin lands on 4.

   a. Find the probability. _____

   b. Explain why the events are dependent.

   _____

2. The first spin lands on 6 and the sum of the results is less than or equal to 10.

   a. Find the probability. _____

   b. Explain why the events are dependent.

   _____

The table shows the population distribution in Ireland in 1996 by age and gender.

	Age 0–20	Age 21–40	Age 41–60	Age 61–80	Age Over 80	Total
Males (in thousands)	620.4	526.8	405.3	212.0	33.0	1797.5
Females (in thousands)	588.3	527.6	400.8	246.3	60.3	1823.3
Total	1208.7	1054.4	806.1	458.3	93.3	3620.8

Use the information in the table to find each probability expressed as a decimal to the nearest hundredth.

3. A randomly selected person is no more than 20 years old, given that the person is male. _____

4. A randomly selected person is female, given that the person is over 80 years old. _____

A bag contains 3 red balls, 7 yellow balls, 5 green balls, and 3 blue balls. Find the probability of selecting these sets without replacement.

5. a red, then a blue, then a green, then a green _____

6. a blue, then a blue, then a blue, then a red _____

Original content Copyright © by Houghton Mifflin Harcourt. Additions and changes to the original content are the responsibility of the instructor.

164

Name _____ Date _____ Class_____

LESSON
23-1 # Using Probability to Make Fair Decisions
Practice and Problem Solving: A/B

Determine whether the method of distributing tickets is fair or not fair.

1. Tickets for female customers only
   _____

2. Three tickets for each customer
   _____

3. Tickets for every other customer
   _____

There are five members in a math club. Determine which methods are fair for choosing one of the members randomly to be the team captain.

4. Assign four of the members one number each and assign one member two numbers.
   _____

5. Assign each member a number on a strip of paper. Choose one of the strips of paper at random from a bowl.
   _____

6. Choose the member who is the oldest.
   _____

Four friends want to go out to dinner. They each want to go to a different restaurant. Which methods are fair for choosing which restaurant to go to?

7. Choose the closest restaurant.

   _____

8. Use a spinner with four equal pie slices, each representing a different restaurant.

   _____

9. Use a spinner with three equal pie slices, representing the top three restaurants.

   _____

10. Write each restaurant name on its own slip of paper and draw a slip of paper at random.

   _____

Original content Copyright © by Houghton Mifflin Harcourt. Additions and changes to the original content are the responsibility of the instructor.
165

Name _____ Date _____ Class_____

LESSON 23-1

Using Probability to Make Fair Decisions

Practice and Problem Solving: C

There are 250 customers who can participate in a prize drawing. Determine whether the method of distributing tickets is fair or not fair.

1. Four tickets for every customer until 100 customers have been given tickets.

   _____

2. Two tickets are given to each of the first 150 customers. Then 2 tickets each for the remaining customers.

   _____

3. One ticket for customers whose last name starts with A–K. One ticket for customers whose last name starts with L–Z.

   _____

Two boys and four girls are on a quiz bowl team. Determine which methods are fair for choosing one of the members randomly to be the team captain.

4. Flip a coin to determine whether the captain will be a boy or girl and write the names of the winning gender on slips of paper. Then choose the captain by drawing a name from a box.

   _____

5. Since there are more girls, assign each girl a number and choose that number at random from a box.

   _____

6. Assign each member a different number from 1–6. Roll a die to determine the winner.

   _____

7. Give each boy two tickets and each girl one ticket. Draw a ticket at random from a box.

   _____

A committee planning a spring dance has three male students, five female students, and two teachers on it. The committee leader will be chosen at random and must be a student. Which methods are fair for choosing the committee leader?

8. A spinner with ten equal-size pie slices, one for each committee member.

   _____

9. Assigning each male student a number between 1 and 3, assigning a female student a number between 7 and 11, and drawing one of these numbers at random from a box.

   _____

10. Assigning each male student two numbers and each female student one number, and drawing one of these numbers at random from a box.

   _____

Name _____ Date _____ Class_____

Analyzing Decisions

Practice and Problem Solving: A/B

A restaurant has a beverage machine that works well 90% of the time. The owners bought a new beverage machine that works well 94% of the time. Each machine is used 50% of the time.

For Problems 1–4, use Bayes' Theorem to find each probability. Round your answer to the nearest tenth of a percent.

1. Old machine malfunctioned   _____

2. New machine malfunctioned   _____

3. Old machine worked well   _____

4. New machine worked well   _____

A small apartment building has two washing machines. Washing Machine A malfunctions 13% of the time. Washing Machine B malfunctions 18% of the time. Washing Machine A is used 60% of the time. Washing Machine B is used 40% of the time.

For problems 5–8, use Bayes' Theorem to find each probability. Round your answer to the nearest tenth of a percent.

5. Machine A malfunctioned.   _____

6. Machine B malfunctioned.   _____

7. Machine A worked well.   _____

8. Machine B worked well.   _____

A prize machine at a festival has a probability of 34% of awarding a customer a ticket for a free meal. An older prize machine has a probability of 45% of awarding a customer a ticket for a free meal. Each machine is used 50% of the time.

9. The next prize drawn is a ticket for a free meal. Use Bayes' Theorem to determine the probability that the new machine awarded this ticket.

_____

Analyzing Decisions
LESSON 23-2
Practice and Problem Solving: C

A bank has a coin counting machine that works well 95% of the time. They have an older coin counting machine that malfunctions 9% of the time. The new machine is used 75% of the time and the old machine is used the remaining percentage of time.

For Problems 1–4, use Bayes' Theorem to find each probability. Round your answer to the nearest tenth of a percent.

1. New machine worked well   _____

2. Old machine malfunctioned   _____

3. New machine malfunction   _____

4. Old machine worked well   _____

Use the following situation for Problems 5–7.

A movie theatre has two popcorn machines. Popcorn Machine A works well 96% of the time. Popcorn Machine B works well 92% of the time. Popcorn Machine A is used 80% of the time. The movie theater owner complains that the popcorn produced has too many kernels that did not pop.

5. Find the probability that Popcorn Machine A was used to make the popcorn   _____

6. Find the probability that Popcorn Machine B was used to make the popcorn   _____

7. The owner blamed Popcorn Machine A for the kernels that did not pop. Was the owner correct in doing so? Explain your answer.   _____

A prize machine at a festival has a probability of 70% of awarding a customer a ticket for a free meal. A new prize machine has a probability of 40% of awarding a customer a ticket for something other than a free meal. The new prize machine is used 80% of the time. Round your answer to the nearest percent.

8. The next prize drawn is a ticket for a free meal. Use Bayes' Theorem to determine the probability that the new machine awarded this ticket.

_____